D1110409

I'd Rather Be Rich

CHOOSING THE LIFE YOU WANT TO LIVE

DISCARDED

I'd Rather Be Rich
CHOOSING THE LIFE YOU WANT TO LIVE

Sheila Leonard CFP

INSOMNIAC PRESS

Copyright © 2008 by Sheila Leonard

All rights reserved. No part of this publication may be reproduced, stored in a retrieval system or transmitted, in any form or by any means, without the prior written permission of the publisher or, in case of photocopying or other reprographic copying, a license from Access Copyright, 1 Yonge Street, Suite 1900, Toronto, Ontario, Canada, M5E 1E5.

Library and Archives Canada Cataloguing in Publication

Leonard, Sheila, 1955-
    I'd rather be rich / Sheila Leonard.

ISBN 978-1-897178-59-1

    1. Self-actualization (Psychology). 2. Success. I. Title.

BF637.S4L463 2008   158.1   C2008-901029-9

The publisher gratefully acknowledges the support of the Department of Canadian Heritage through the Book Publishing Industry Development Program.

Printed and bound in Canada

Insomniac Press
192 Spadina Avenue, Suite 403
Toronto, Ontario, Canada, M5T 2C2
www.insomniacpress.com

Canada

This book is dedicated to
my friend Sandi Lee, and
my brother T.J. Leonard.

You asked for it!

Acknowledgements

I must start with a huge hug to my friend, Theresa Corcoran. She invited me to my very first workshop back in 1990. Thank you for having the courage to take a risk. This book, and so much of the past 15 years of my life, would not have been possible without the wonderful teachers who have touched my life. Christopher Moon, you gave me the encouragement to become a teacher myself. Chuck Spezzano, Ph.D., your development of the Psychology of Vision has changed the lives of so many. Kelly Tobey, thank you for teaching me to say "No." Henri McKinnon, thank you for never giving up on me. Heather Clarke, thank you for introducing me to God. Sam Leonard, thank you for providing such a beautiful and inspiring place, Hacienda Mosaico, in which to start writing my book. Mike and Sandi Lee, you continue to inspire and challenge and support me—with all my heart "Thank You!" Rebecca Graham, thank you for being my partner in this work and for always encouraging me to dig a little deeper. Isabella Ammirati and Donna Sellers: you each showed me what real support and team work looks like. I really couldn't have written the book without you. Erin Michie, your energy, love, and enthusiasm really moved this project to completion. You are a great member of our Master Mind group. Gillian Urbankiewicz—thank you for your patience, understanding, and remarkable attention to detail. To Inktree Marketing, Chapters/Indigo, *The Calgary Sun*, and Insomniac Press, thank you for creating "The Write Stuff" publishing competition, without which this book would not have been completed. And to all the very special friends and friends of friends who voted for this book to be published, THANK YOU! I am so very blessed, abundant, and grateful.

CONTENTS

INTRODUCTION

This is a life planning book and I'm a Certified Financial Planner. As a financial planner, I have noticed a few things about people and their financial goals. People have money, or not, because of how they think. I have spent time helping people consolidate debt and they just created more. I have helped people set up a savings program, but they just found more things they wanted to buy. I have clearly seen that accumulating wealth is of no value if it is not helping to build a life that is wealthy on all levels. Being rich is not about the amount of money you have; it is about how you feel about and use your money. I speak more about what I mean by the word "rich" in Week 1, but before we look more closely at the concept, I'd like to share some of my experience.

I entered the business of financial planning because I wanted to help people become wealthy, so they would have more resources and make better choices for their happiness. What I have learned from advising people for over a decade is that before they are willing and able to make lasting changes in their behaviours, they have to change their mindset. What needs to change is people's minds. The problem is that neither I nor anyone else can change another person's mind. It is a job for the individual. That's why this is a workbook. The intention of this book is to help you change your mind—essentially, how you think about the parts of your life that are not working as well as you would like. I know that once this is accomplished, your actions will automatically change in the direction of greater wealth, health, and happiness.

I began writing this introduction while sitting in beautiful and sunny Puerto Vallarta, Mexico. I was not just on vacation; I was working (if you can call sitting by the pool working). I was in a fabulous 6,000 square foot villa with my friends Sandi and Mike Lee. Rufi, an employee of Sandi and Mike's, was taking immaculate care of the place and our every culinary desire. The villa was located right on the beach and the sunsets were a kaleidoscope of colour.

What an exciting time I had getting there! I'm not talking about the plane ride or the wild taxi drivers of Puerto Vallarta. I am talking about the creative process I used in producing this experience. This was not just chance or great luck—it was an experience I consciously chose. And if I can do it, so can you! This book will show you how to consciously create your experience and guide you on your journey to where you would rather be.

A few years ago, I went down to visit my friends who had recently moved to Puerto Vallarta and I loved it! While sharing rum and Cokes at The Paradise Burger, Mike asked me if I would consider moving down. At the time, the idea felt like a fantasy, but I kept my mind open and chewed on the concept. Perhaps I couldn't live there full-time, but a few months a year might be possible. As I played with the idea, I began to visit Sandi and Mike more often—I'm currently averaging six weeks each year.

I had some ideas about how I could live full-time in Puerto Vallarta, but nothing that really convinced me. It still seemed like a fantasy. However, since I was coming from Canadian winters, my love of the warm climate grew. About a year and a half later, in the frosty temperatures of late autumn, I was sitting in a business planning session. In a creative flash, I had the thought: "Why don't I write a book in Puerto Vallarta? It would give me the experience of what it would be like to live and work in Mexico." Immediately, my body was tingling: I felt the excitement. I knew it was the thing to do. I didn't really know why I wanted to write a book. A few people encouraged me to do it, but it had never been a burning desire. Although, I must admit, it fit with my dream of many years of being a teacher. I pitched the book to my managers as a marketing idea, and to my delight they didn't try to stop me.

I had many grand experiences during my first month in Mexico. With great discipline I wrote over 100 pages. I even talked to a possible publisher and felt I had really made some headway. At first I thought I was just going to make a few copies for my friends and possibly some workshop participants because I felt that the manuscript that was in progress was very private.

Back home in Canada, I lost interest in the project. The time, effort, and financing needed to finish my fledgling book seemed too overwhelming. I got busy with my life and career and left the manuscript sitting in a drawer. About six months later, my dear friend Shelley Allen called and asked if I had entered "The Write Stuff" competition. (It's a contest similar to American Idol for authors, run in southern Alberta.) I told her that I had heard about it, but that it was for authors—I was a financial planner. I argued that the program was for novels, not self-help books. Thankfully she didn't listen to me. She made me promise to enter the contest.

Once I give my word, I always follow through. At the 11th hour, I spent all of ten minutes entering the contest by cutting and pasting from my manuscript. Definitely not expecting anything, I thought, "Now I can tell Shelley that I entered the contest, and that will be the end of it."

Well, I was completely flabbergasted when Inktree Marketing called to congratulate me on being one of the ten finalists—out of 764 entries! Once the judges had chosen the top ten, the general public was able to vote for one person, once a day, online. There were press pictures to take, a count-down to the top five finalists, and then an evening to an-nounce the winner. Throughout the process, I was very fortunate to have many friends and peers who not only voted themselves, but also had their network of friends and family vote for me, and so it grew. In the end, I won a $35,000 pub-lishing contract, gave several radio and television interviews, and spent another month in *bonita* Puerto Vallarta working on my book.

This is how the book works. Within this chronicle are the Principles of Creation. Following the Principles are exam-ples in italics from the story of creating this book that you just read:

1. Have a dream. Make it as wild and crazy and fabulous as you can imagine.

When Mike asked me to consider living in Puerto Val-larta, it felt like a fantasy, but I did not dismiss it. I started to think about ways to make it possible.

2. Be open to the idea of that dream or fantasy becoming a reality.

I played with and investigated the idea. I kept open to the possibility.

3. Be on the look out for ways of accomplishing even small parts, or your entire dream.

Perhaps I couldn't live there full-time, but a few months a year might be possible.

4. Support comes in many different forms. Be open, acknowledge it, and be grateful.

It was in the most unlikely place, a business planning session, that I first opened my mind to the idea of writing a book while sunning in Mexico. Shelley pushed me to enter the publishing contest and so many people voted for me that I won the contract.

5. As ideas come, pay attention to how they feel.

Immediately upon getting the idea to write the book, my body was tingling. I felt the excitement.

6. Once an idea creates a strong emotion (such as either excitement or fear), commit to taking action on it as soon as possible.

Yes! I knew it was the thing to do. With great discipline I wrote over 100 pages and felt I had really made some headway. Once I agreed to enter the contest, I followed through and did it.

7. Follow the energy of the project. If "all systems are go," keep moving forward. If huge resistance is encountered, let it go. Have patience for gestation. Be on the lookout for a new way through.

About a year and a half later, I was sitting in a business planning session....

In a creative flash....

I got busy with my life and career and left the manuscript sitting in a drawer....

It took time for an idea to emerge on how to work and play in Puerto Vallarta. Once the original draft was completed, the manuscript sat in a drawer for six months before the contest was created.

8. Know that personal issues and beliefs may get in the way. Clear them up.

If there is something that you truly want, but it is not being manifested in your life, it is only because you are blocking it. Look at why you might be afraid to have what you say you want. What might you lose by having it? You always have what you allow yourself to have in your life, so something has to change internally to allow your new desire.

The time, effort, and financing to realize my fledgling project seemed too overwhelming. I stopped pushing, but kept open enough to investigate my lack of confidence, resources, etc. Through a process of many stop, starts, and new ideas, this book is finally in your hands.

9. As personal issues are cleared out of the way, the next nudge towards the dream will appear. Pay attention to the nudges and keep moving forward.

It was after clearing personal issues that Shelley encouraged me to enter the contest. Later, my friend Erin Michie helped me with the final draft.

10. Keep dreaming. Dreaming helps you have a fascinating experience of life.

It still seemed like a fantasy, but coming from Canadian winters, my love of the warm climate grew. I kept going back to Puerto Vallarta several times a year. I kept going back to the manuscript and never gave up. During the process, I had many new and exciting experiences such as press, radio, and TV interviews.

These are principles and not steps. Steps imply that you follow an order. Not so with principles. Number 8, "Personal issues/beliefs," can get in your way right from the beginning. Number 5, "Pay attention to your feelings," must be considered throughout the entire process. As we move along, these principles are encountered in almost all sections. Write out these principles yourself and post them on your bathroom mirror to remind you of their importance each day. You can also find them in the Tool Box at the back of the book.

I'd Rather Be Rich was created to help people, just like you, who want to get more out of life. If you are tired or feeling stuck, this book is for you! If you feel good, but want to get even more out of life than you already have, this book is for you! If you want more abundance, more adventure, better relationships or a better world, this book is for you! Even if you are tired of goal setting, this book is for you.

But if you want other people or your situation to change without your having to, this book is not for you. For your world to change, you and you alone must do the changing. You must change what you think about, change what you believe, and change what you do. As you change internally, you will act differently in your external world, and your world will change along with you.

I didn't use the words "simple" or "easy" in the book title. I am suspicious of being sold a quick fix formula or a pill that claims to work for everyone. Real, lasting change is not always that easy and it's possible to get disappointed and quit before you get where you want to go. I want you to get there! I have designed this book to be a course, a workshop, and a process. I call it a road map because I will show you the way, but will not tell you where to go. When you use a road map, you are always free to choose where you want to go, which way to go, and even whether you want to leave home. I use the analogy of taking a road trip, because frankly, most people spend more time planning their vacations than they do their lives. I am going to ask you to spend 15 minutes a day creating the life of your dreams. Interested?

WEEK 1
A Road Map to Where You'd Rather Be

Famous comedian Sophie Tucker said, "Honey, I've been rich, and I've been poor, and rich is better." Having had both experiences, I'd have to say I wholeheartedly agree with her. But just what is being rich? It is different for everyone. For some it means owning their own home, or providing for their children's education. For others it's the ability to travel in luxury. Others would like to quit their current job and find a career that inspires them. It could mean living in an exotic country. It often contains a certain dollar figure. What rich means to someone earning $30,000 per year is very different from what it means to a person earning $500,000 per year.

As you make more money, you keep raising the bar. Being rich is not about the amount of money you have, it is about how you feel about and use money. It is not so much about *being* rich, it is about *feeling* rich, and for many, it does take some money to feel rich.

To feel rich I need to have a balance of security and freedom. I want to know that I have the financial freedom to do whatever I want, whenever I want. I want to make my decisions based on what I desire, not what I think I can afford. I also want to feel financially secure by knowing that the financial freedom I have today will be there throughout my life. Being rich is about money and it is not about money: it is both. Money cannot buy you happiness, but living without it limits your experiences and your choices in life.

Feeling rich is also about having a full, rewarding experience of life. To me, this means feeling peace, happiness, and contentment. I want to have my life full of passionate, loving, gentle, and honest people. I want to continually expand my knowledge and experiences. I love to try new things and explore new places. I want to be surrounded with beauty. I want to begin and end each day in gratitude. I want it all!

In this book, I have included lines for you to write on. I want you to try to completely fill each and every line. If you need more space, great, get a journal to continue the exercises, but it's important that you fill all the space provided. If you run out of thoughts to fill the lines, stop and ask yourself the question again. More information will come.

What does being rich look and feel like to you?

_____

_____

_____

_____

_____

_____

_____

_____

_____

_____

_____

_____

My relationship with money and financial planning started early in my life. My parents encouraged me to give and to save. I had my first bank account at the age of five.

Although it didn't contain very much money, I always felt proud and grown up when I walked into the bank and deposited my savings. As a youngster, I developed positive feelings toward money. I saw the benefits of compound interest and watched my money grow. By the time I was 12, I had learned how to budget. My parents gave me an allowance of $5 every two weeks to buy most of my clothes and pay for entertainment. I also used that allowance to buy presents, give at Sunday school each week, and save a small portion for the future.

I often hear parents complaining about how their children handle money. They say things like, "They think money comes out of a hole in the wall (ATM's)." These people do not seem to realize that they have taught their children about money through their example.

I have clients who learned this lesson the hard way. Their son, Dale, was full of grandiose ideas and expected his parents to bail him out of every failed business venture. Their daughter, Vanessa, just couldn't get a handle on a career she was willing to work at. Dale and Vanessa, already in their early 30's, did not take responsibility for their lives or for their decisions because they had never had to. Their parents were constantly dishing out cash. After many incidents, I finally convinced the parents to admit and release their own motivation (guilt) for constantly rescuing their children, and to really look at what they were teaching them.

The parents then made it clear that the hand outs were over. It took a year of struggle for Dale and Vanessa to be convinced of their parents' commitment, but after a year, they were well on their way to becoming self-supporting.

If you have children, I encourage you to start teaching them about money as soon as possible. As you will see later in this book, our earliest money memories have an amazing impact throughout our lives. Make them good ones!

One of my early money memories involves my father. As he was coming out of the grocery store, he saw a roll of bills just lying on the ground. He undid the elastic band and counted out the money. There was enough to cover his mortgage payment that was due in just a few days. He was tempted, but then he looked over at my sister and I in the car and thought "What do I want to teach my children?" He turned around and took the money to the customer service desk. While he was waiting, a young man came rushing in. He was frantic. He had just lost his entire two weeks' pay. It had been rolled up in a rubber band. The young man was so grateful for my father's honesty and integrity. Dad felt good about himself, too. Our whole family learned a valuable lesson that stays with each of us to this day. As you set the intention to help teach your children positive lessons about money, be conscious that they will follow what you do, far more than what you say. Know that as you follow your new road map, you will learn remarkable lessons to pass on to your children.

Matching your actions with your words is an essential part of living with integrity. When you do what you say you will, you not only develop trust in yourself, but others place their trust in you, as well. When you do not do what you say you will, you lose your self-esteem and the esteem of others.

I originally trained as a bookkeeper and an accountant. It seemed like a natural choice, as I had always been well organized and good at math. It may have been a natural choice (the path of least resistance or effort), but it wasn't one that inspired me. I slept through every accounting class. Every assignment was dull and boring. What was I to do? I even tried taking classes to help figure out what I'd be good at and to introduce me to different options. Still nothing caught my attention. I had no dream, no vision, nothing, zippo.

At the age of 29, I finally gave up trying to find a new career. I sat down with myself and looked at my options. I decided that I could not live one day past age 45 as an accountant. My goal became to retire from accounting within the next 16 years. Then I looked at the possible ways I could achieve this goal. I could go back to university, get a degree, and then earn more money after school. Or, I could just start saving money for my retirement immediately. Like many people, I opted for what seemed the easiest route—I started a savings plan. I decided to maximize my Registered Retirement Savings Plan (RRSP) each year to have my savings earn 10% annually. I also saved any additional money I earned such as interest, tax refunds, gifts of money, bonuses, and so on. Whatever was left, I got to spend freely. I showed my plan to a Chartered Accountant friend. He scoffed at it, saying it was too big a plan, and that I would never do it. Thank you, Cam. Little did you know that I had started saving $100 per month because someone told me "you'll never do it." For me, being told "you can't" was a great motivator.

At first it was challenging to live within my budget. With each purchase, I asked myself, "Do I want this, or do I want to be retired?" I was committed. I kept choosing retirement. I quickly saw the universe support my dreams. Seeming miracles happened. Originally, I had been making $24,000 a year. Seven years later, I was making $60,000. I stayed committed to my goals and had even more money to enhance my life at the same time. I travelled around the world and still kept within my plan. At 37, within eight years of setting my goal, I quit being an accountant. I had achieved my dream in half the time!

Now, I knew that I didn't have enough money saved to retire, but the goal of no longer being an accountant had been achieved. My path became a little clearer and I then decided that I wanted to become a workshop leader. For five years I lived a grand life of travelling, spending time with my family, and continuing my spiritual journey. I led weekly classes in "A Course in Miracles," ran a workshop promotions company, and even helped start a spa and wellness centre. And then the vision became even more clear. At 44, I saw an advertisement for financial planning. Everything inside me said, "Yes, this is my vocation!" I never wanted to retire again. Today my work continually inspires me, and I love it.

I am now a Certified Financial Planner focused on helping my clients to make their dreams come true. I also lead workshops that combine both my financial and spiritual knowledge and gifts. I have been saddened to learn how few people have dreams and goals that stretch past next year. This supports the saying that "wealthy people plan for the next generation while poor people plan for Saturday night."

Wealth and vision are travel companions. The greater and more detailed your vision, the richer your life will be. And that is why I have written this book. I am not a psychologist, but from my own life journey and the many gifted teachers who have inspired me, I have learned to stretch my limited thinking, take action, and achieve a lifestyle envied by many. This book is an accumulation of what I have learned in the past 20 years of workshops, books, lectures and one-on-one training. I know that it is possible for everyone to make their dreams come true and I want to help you do just that. I invite you to choose as much happiness as you can handle and to choose to be where you'd rather be!

In 2002, I was invited to join a Master Mind Group. It was an extremely powerful process for me. Every week I had to come to the meeting with the answer to what I believe is one of the most important questions we can ask: "What do I want?" Certainly I had asked myself that question periodically, but never with such consistency. From it, I began to gain clarity about what was truly important to me—not what others wanted or expected of me, but what my heart was truly crying out for. Because you have picked up this book, I know that to listen to your heart's call is also your quest. Your heart calls you to live in a way that fills you, fulfills you, and creates happiness, contentment, and peace.

I am going to ask you some tough questions. Think about them and write down the first thoughts that enter your mind. Don't restrict yourself to what you believe is possible—throw open the doors to your wildest thoughts and dreams. If any negative thoughts pop into your mind like: "This is dumb, this is impossible," write them in the margin beside the desire that gave rise to these reactions. It is important to write down those thoughts, as it is a way to acknowledge them and not suppress them. Then, choose which you want to believe. If you hang on to a belief that something is impossible, you will be right. If you are open to the possibility of changing that belief in order to have what you truly want, you will be right, too.

Most of the things worth doing in the world
had been declared impossible before they were done.
- Louis D. Brandeis, 1856-1941, American judge

Many of you are so busy with schedules, careers, families and meeting other people's needs that you don't take the time to ask: "What do I really want?" It's time to practice. If you get stuck for an answer, try looking at what is in your life that you *don't* want. That will show you what you *do* want. For example, it may be that you feel stressed at work and you don't want that. Instead you may want to feel secure, relaxed, and even have fun at work. Wouldn't that be better? Another option is to replace the word "want" with the phrase "I would enjoy…" Don't worry about how to achieve these desires; the first step is just letting them become conscious. The means and method will emerge later.

I want _____

I want _____

I want _____

I want _____

I want _____

I want _____

I want _____

I want _____

I want _____

I want _____

What kind of a day do you want to have? What do you want to happen today?

I want _____

I want _____

I want _____

I want _____

I want _____

What do you want to happen this week?

I want _____

I want _____

I want _____

I want _____

I want _____

Where do you want to vacation? What do you want that vacation to be like?

I want _____
I want _____
I want _____
I want _____
I want _____

What could happen next month that would truly excite and fill you with anticipation?

I want _____
I want _____
I want _____
I want _____
I want _____

Your perfect job would have what qualities? What would you be doing?

I want _____
I want _____
I want _____
I want _____
I want _____

Whether you have a life partner, or not, what are the qualities that would make that person fabulous, in your eyes?

I want _____

I want _____

I want _____

I want _____

I want _____

I want _____

I want _____

I want _____

I want _____

I want _____

Looking at yourself, what qualities would you like to develop and enhance?

I want _____

I want _____

I want _____

I want _____

I want _____

Looking at your children, pets, and friends, what changes would you like to see? What kind of people do you want to spend your time with? Doing what?

I want _____

I want _____

I want _____

I want _____

I want _____

How would you like to spend your spare time, if you had any?

I want _____

I want _____

I want _____

I want _____

I want _____

Looking at your financial situation, what do you want?

I want _____

I want _____

I want _____

I want _____

I want _____

Looking forward to next year, if money, time, energy and other people's needs were not a factor, what would you like your life to look like?

I want _____

I want _____

I want _____

I want _____

I want _____

I want _____

I want _____

I want _____

I want _____

I want _____

How did you feel as you completed your list? Was it fun to think about all the things you could add to your life, or did you feel uncomfortable? Perhaps greedy? Or overwhelmed? Or guilty? Did any thoughts arise about deserving these things? Do you believe you have a right to good things in your life or do you believe you have to earn them? Are there limits to your receiving? Take a few moments to write about the feelings that arose answering the previous questions and the possible reasons for them.

_____

_____

_____

_____

_____

_____

_____

_____

_____

_____

_____

_____

Reviewing your list, can you see any themes? Are most of your wants about accumulating possessions, or about having better relationships? Do your desires require more time, or money, or energy? Is there a specific area of your life that seems to want more attention? Do any other trends pop out for you?

_____

_____

_____

_____

_____

_____

_____

_____

_____

_____

_____

_____

You have started plotting possible destinations for your journey. Congratulations on choosing to be where you'd rather be!

The Road Log to Where You'd Rather Be

Treat this book as a weekly course. Set up a time each week, just as if you were taking a driver's education class. Each week, read only one chapter and do the exercises. Don't jump ahead! There are 21 weeks in this program. If you speed ahead, most of the information will be lost in a relatively short time. Just think of the last great book you read. How much of it do you really remember? How did you use the information in that book? How did it enhance your life? If you are like most people, reading alone does not create much change, but adding action does. We are going to start taking action by writing each day. **For the next week, start each day by spending 15 minutes writing and reflecting on what you want in your life.**

If you don't have one already, buy a journal in which to do this writing. In time, it will be a great resource to see how far you have travelled. I call it the "Road Log for the Journey to Where You'd Rather Be."

I had been told the benefits of journalling for years, but I never set aside the time to do it. In the beginning, I was not very good at visualization, meditation, or going inside myself. What worked for me was writing. As I would get upset about something, I learned that writing it down and asking myself questions created clarity for me. But I only made writing important after I had tried everything else. I once remember asking my brother to destroy my journals if anything should happen to me, because they were full of all my struggles. I tried writing "morning pages" (from Julia Cameron's book *The Artist's Way*) of whatever was in my mind. I tried writing daily lists of gratitude. Nothing was consistent. I don't think I ever lasted more than a few weeks.

What has worked for me is committing myself to writing about what I want every day. I see a big payoff from my spending my time this way. I am creating what I want, and it takes less than 15 minutes a day. My journals are no longer filled with frustration: they are filled with creative and stimulating ideas. They are filled with dreams that have come true and those that are on their way. My journals are filled with passion, and so am I.

As you start taking 15 minutes a day to write about what you want, you will notice that you will naturally start creating more of what you want. Instead of forcing yourself to take action or change, you will notice that you are inspired to move. You will be filled with the desire and the energy to shift the details of your life. Things will just start getting handled. There may be a huge shift, or it could be subtle enough that it may take a month to really notice the difference. Some people start eating better and exercising. Some improve their relationships and some start taking better care of themselves—all within the first week. Just start and you will be amazed. It helps to get a beautiful journal for your Road Log. Have fun and watch the results!

During your 15 minutes a day, rewrite each of your 75 wants in positive sentences. Never write, "I don't want." Whatever you focus on expands, so if you focus on not wanting conflict you will create more conflict. The word "conflict" is a word with tremendous energy behind it. Focus instead on wanting peace and you will achieve more of that. For example, Mother Teresa said she would never attend a rally against war, but she would attend a peace rally any time.

Whenever we fight against anything we give it more focus, more energy, and more power. Negative energy creates negative reactions and results.

How do the two words, peace and conflict, feel in your body when you think of each of them? Peace feels much better than conflict or war. Focusing on peace makes us feel better. The better we feel, the more we will like what we are creating.

So, if you don't want to spend Christmas with the in-laws, write out where you'd rather be. "I want to spend Christmas at home." Or, write out what experience you would rather have. "I want a quiet Christmas filled with music and good books." As you rewrite these wants, put them into positive, present tense sentences. You might use phrases such as:

I see myself_____

I choose_____

I'm open to_____

I know_____

Pay special attention to how you feel as you write out each statement. Does the idea of this desire uplift you, terrify you, or do you have any emotion about it at all? In a different colour of pen, write out the predominant feeling beside each statement. If you have any idea what thoughts or beliefs are connected with these feelings, also write them down.

Your desires may change through this process. You may also see the feeling attached to a specific desire change during the week. Be curious. Ask yourself questions. What do you notice? Look for themes. Why do you want these things? What are the underlying benefits of having them? Going back to our Christmas with the in-laws example, perhaps you don't like the atmosphere at their house. What don't you like? How would you like to see it change? Do you really want to exclude them from your life, or would you prefer to have a better experience with them? What underlying issue is driving your desire to be alone? For some of the more meaningful desires, try just focusing on one for your 15 minutes of journalling in the morning. Notice what you learn as you spend the time paying attention to just one desire.

From this point on, keep your Daily Road Log and write about what you want, each and every day. As you accomplish each goal, reward yourself in any way that appeals to you. Ensure that your reward is not an indulgence that sabotages you. One piece of chocolate could be a reward for meeting your weight goal, but the whole box would be an indulgence. After accomplishing your goal, move on to your next desire. Often you may find that you are working on several goals at a time. Don't limit yourself. Just keep going.

Do the above writing exercise for a minimum of seven days, before continuing to the next chapter. In the future, it will be a valued treasure map. Also, remember to write out the ten Principles of Creation and post them on your bathroom mirror. By keeping it in front of you everyday, it will serve as a reminder, and will initiate continued focus.

WEEK 2
Explore Possible Destinations

How was your week? Did you start making any progress towards what you say you want? Have you achieved any of your desires? How did the process feel? Was it easy or hard to focus 15 minutes a day on yourself? Were you tempted to miss a day? What else did you notice?

_____

_____

_____

_____

_____

_____

_____

_____

_____

_____

_____

_____

_____

_____

Do you make a grocery list before driving to the store? I have found that if I go to the grocery store without a list, I make impulse purchases, I spend more money, and I end up throwing out some of what I bought because I can't use it. I might strain my back carrying more than I need, and I always forget something and have to go back to the grocery store—what a waste of time, money, and energy! When I go with a list, I spend less and have to make fewer trips to the store. I free up time and money for things that are far more important and inspiring for me.

Life is like grocery shopping. If you write down what you want, you will get far less of what you don't want and you will remember what is essential. It speeds up your progress towards your desires and helps create more happiness and fulfillment in the process. The intention of this process is to support and inspire you to spend 15 minutes a day—each and every day—focused directly on what you want. Notice what happens. It is a simple exercise, but you must carry it out to succeed.

Next, I would like to explore your wish list a little more deeply. Let's answer similar questions from the perspective of what you really *need* to live a happier, healthier, and more fulfilling life—a life where you can't wait to get out of bed to enjoy the day.

I need _____

I need _____

I need _____

I need _____

I need _____

I need _____

I need _____

What kind of a day do you need to have for your peace of mind? For your happiness?

I need _____
I need _____
I need _____
I need _____
I need _____
I need _____
I need _____

What do you need to happen this week for your peace of mind? What would make this week meaningful?

I need _____
I need _____
I need _____
I need _____
I need _____
I need _____
I need _____

Where do you need to vacation to truly rejuvenate? What do you need your vacation to be like to enable you to successfully renew your energy? What do you need to truly value and appreciate your vacation?

I need _____
I need _____
I need _____
I need _____
I need _____
I need _____
I need _____

What do you need to happen next month? What would truly excite and fill you with anticipation?

I need _____

I need _____

I need _____

I need _____

I need _____

I need _____

I need _____

Your perfect job would have certain qualities. What would you be doing?

I need _____

I need _____

I need _____

I need _____

I need _____

I need _____

I need _____

What are the qualities you feel you need in a spouse or partner? Answer whether you have one or not.

I need _____

I need _____

I need _____

I need _____

I need _____

I need _____

I need _____

Looking at yourself, what qualities do you need to develop to live a happy and fulfilling life? What qualities would give you more self-respect and pride?

I need _____

I need _____

I need _____

I need _____

I need _____

I need _____

I need _____

Looking at your children, pets, and friends, what changes need to happen for you to enjoy their company more fully? What kind of people do you need to spend your time with for peace of mind? Doing what?

I need _____

I need _____

I need _____

I need _____

I need _____

I need _____

I need _____

How do you need to spend your spare time to fully relax and rejuvenate?

I need _____

I need _____

I need _____

I need _____

I need _____

I need _____

I need _____

Looking at your financial situation, what do you need to achieve to feel financially secure?

I need _____

I need _____

I need _____

I need _____

I need _____

I need _____

I need _____

Looking forward to next year, if money, time, energy, and other people's needs were not a factor, what would you need in your life to be ecstatically happy and to live a life full of meaning and purpose that you would be proud of?

I need _____

I need _____

I need _____

I need _____

I need _____

I need _____

I need _____

Now, how do you feel after completing this list? Do your needs feel more important than wants? What trends do you see here? What are the changes or similarities between what you want and what you need? Are any further feelings of guilt, greed, or unworthiness emerging?

_____

_____

_____

_____

_____

_____

_____

_____

_____

_____

_____

You will notice that I phrased the questions along the lines of what you need to be happy, to have peace of mind, to be fulfilled, relaxed, healthy, etc. Why? Because most of us think that our needs are only what we must have to survive. This program is not about surviving. It is about thriving! There are things you need in order to thrive: make them important. Without them life is boring, hard, and, in my opinion, not worth living. If you are not living your life for yourself, who or what are you living it for? Really, stop and think about that question. Reviewing your life, who are you living it for?

_____

_____

_____

_____

_____

_____

_____

Is it your parents? I know that if you asked them, they would say they just want you to be happy. Is it your spouse, partner, or significant other? If your happiness is not important to them, why are they in your life?

Is it your children? I know that you want them to be happy, but you must be a role model by taking care of yourself to truly teach them. Otherwise, they will be tempted to take up the role of a Sacrificer, who does everything for everyone else, or an Indulger, who has no thought for anyone else. As you look deeper, you may find that the desire for money is driving your behaviour. Is it truly creating long-term happiness for you? Perhaps you may be swayed by the need for others' approval. When you are attached to getting something from another, you create your own prison. It is only when we consciously choose those things that bring us the greatest happiness that we begin to become the gift we were meant to be to our families, our friends, and our world.

Now, I know that some people argue that focusing on personal happiness and fulfillment is self-indulgent: Nothing could be further from the truth. When you focus on what you really want and need, you are filling up your emotional well with positive thoughts. As your thoughts improve, you will become happy in healthier ways and you will automatically stop the unhealthy behaviours, indulgences, and activities that don't really satisfy you. Have you ever noticed how you eat more or starve yourself when you are upset? That's an un-healthy indulgence! It hurts you and it hurts those who love you.

As you fill your emotional well with positive thoughts and activities, you will feel better. As you continue to hold a better feeling, you will automatically start to attract better re-sults in your life and you will naturally have a more positive and happy outlook to give to the world. Taking care of your-self is the single best way to care for others.

Unhappiness is just too big a sacrifice! Everyone deserves to be happy. More than ever, our world needs people who ra-diate happiness. I believe that it is our ultimate purpose, our goal, and our divine birthright. I am not talking about the short-term high that comes from indulgence. Often we choose pleasure instead of happiness. I am encouraging long-term happiness that is stable and remains throughout the ups and downs of daily life.

Commitment to the Journey

I, _____, hereby commit to my happiness. I commit to spending at least 15 minutes per day creating my happiness. I commit to listening to myself. Each _____ (pick a day of the week), I will meet with myself and spend time reviewing this road map. I com-mit to having what I want in my life. I commit to being where I'd rather be. I commit to completing this book.

Now, I would like you to choose a reward for finishing this book; not just reading it, but actually working through it. I acknowledge that it will take persistence and discipline to keep moving forward. Choose a reward that will help support your commitment. Choose a reward that will make it almost impossible to be tempted to miss even a day. Make it grand: a home renovation, an exotic vacation, an expensive piece of jewellery, golf clubs, etc. Something that when you are tempted to slack off, you can say "Do I want to miss a day or do I want _____?" Instead of something physical, you may choose a new situation. For example, to be retired or to be in a new career. Your reward needs to be something bigger than you would currently allow yourself to have and it must be just for you. If you know you could cheat and still give your reward to yourself, even if you don't follow through on this commitment, it isn't big enough. What has long been a burning desire? If you haven't already done so, please fill in the blank area with your reward.

Did you have trouble making this commitment? If so, it is a great time to start looking at why you can't (*can't* is really *won't*) commit to yourself and your happiness. What could possibly be more important? Devoting 15 minutes a day to yourself is about valuing yourself, and the more you value yourself, the more you give to yourself, and the more others will value and give to you. Your world mirrors how you treat yourself.

Write about what commitment means to you. How does it help you? How does it hurt you? Write about your resistance to committing to having what you need, want, and desire in your life.

_____

_____

_____

_____

_____

_____

———————————————————————
———————————————————————
———————————————————————
———————————————————————
———————————————————————
———————————————————————
———————————————————————

Because freedom is such a huge need for me, I used to have an issue with commitment. Finally, I realized that commitment is giving my whole heart, not being locked into something for all of eternity—at all cost. Never get so attached to achieving a goal that you betray your own personal values, or the values of the people you care about. For an extreme example, you wouldn't go out and steal a shiny new car just because you were committed to having one. That would betray the values and laws of your community, hurt your loved ones, and (I'm hoping) go against your personal values, too. You get back what you put out. Holding onto fear, lack, or deceit will eventually create more of those things in your life.

Make your commitments to and about yourself. Make them guidelines and not rules. Use them to help you get through the tough places where you may be tempted to give up. Use them to be aware of your choices. Commit to your happiness and fulfillment. Commit to creating your own version of heaven on earth.

Commitment is the FREEDOM
to be where you would rather be.

Sitting on a beautiful beach in sunny Mexico, a woman remarked that she couldn't move forward in her life because there were so many things that she wanted to do, she just couldn't choose. What she was really saying was, "I'm too scared to make a choice." Here she was, retired in her early 40's, but lost. Money was not the problem, (it never is). Her relationship was a mess and she would not make a decision about it. She was waiting for her husband to change, but she wasn't willing to change herself. She just sat around in her misery, trying to make the best of it. She was afraid to make the choices that she needed to and wasn't committed to herself, or anyone else — she was stuck!

The problem is not that there are too many choices; it is that we won't choose. It is like having your feet firmly planted on either side of a picket fence. You can't move and something is irritating your rear end. To move forward towards happiness, all it takes is to make a choice. It doesn't have to be a lifelong choice. If you decide to go to New York, but half way there you decide you would be happier in Miami, you get to change your mind. It doesn't even matter if it's the right choice. By making the wrong choice, you will actually be able to make the right choice more quickly than by making no choice at all. And you can make more than one choice. You can work on several goals at the same time. This is putting together your dream destination, or where you'd rather be. It doesn't matter what you choose, just choose something. The rest will fall into place.

Affirmations

Throughout this book, I will be offering you affirmations to use each week. Affirmations are strong, positive sentences that you can use to set the intention and direction of your day, your week, or your life. Start each day with the suggested affirmation or choose one for yourself. Say them out loud whenever possible, and in your mind, as you need to. The more emotion you can put behind the words, the better. Try saying your affirmation first thing in the morning and last thing at night. You could make a habit of saying your affirmation whenever you brush your teeth, walk through a door, or get in your car. If you want to increase the power of your commitment, increase the number of times you say your statement each day. Five or six times a day will help keep it at the front of your mind. I keep little sticky notes at various locations in my home and office to remind me.

Affirmation: I choose to be happy!

Adding an element of visualization to your affirmation will make it even stronger. So, as you say this week's affirmation, take a moment to focus on something or someone you feel happy being around.

This week use the above affirmation or create one for yourself; either way, start using one. Continue spending 15 minutes each day writing and reflecting on what you want, need, and enjoy in your Road Log. How do you feel about the desires you wrote down? Take another look at your lists and notice what you are currently choosing in your life, instead of the desires you have written about. Be interested in why there is a difference. Pay particular attention to what is happening in your life and what you think about. You can write about that in your morning entry, too.

You are in the process of becoming more conscious. You are beginning to move from the autopilot or cruise control of your subconscious and are taking back your power. You are starting to use your road map.

WEEK 3
Who Needs A Roadmap Anyway?

Take care to get what you like,
or you will be forced to like what you get.
— George Bernard Shaw, 1856-1950, critic and playwright

As reported in *Advisor's Edge* magazine, July 2005 from RBC's 2005 RSP Survey:
- 66% of Canadians surveyed want to retire before they turn 65.
- 79% who are not yet retired do not have a retirement plan.
- 59% of those not yet retired say they are behind in saving for retirement.

Would you set out on a cross-country road trip without a map? Life, lived without a plan, is like driving without a map. It's alright to drive without a map, if you are going to keep driving over familiar roads and never change your view or experiences. But if you want to travel on new roads (and have new experiences in your life) it's easier with a map. Without a map, who knows where you will end up? You might not like it! I firmly believe that all of our lives can be better with a road map. It's the direct route to where you'd rather be.

The famous definition of insanity is doing the same things you've always done and expecting different results.

With so many books on goal setting, why do so few people use them? Many think it is because of laziness. Others believe that you will only change if the present conditions are too painful. Both are about avoiding pain and taking the path of least resistance. I believe that most people do not change because their unconscious goal is to safely get to death.

Change can be intimidating because the devil you know is better than the one you don't. If you are surviving in the current situation, why rock the boat? As you make the decision to move towards a more passionate life, various fears will present themselves and so will various excuses. Let's look at a couple of excuses about why not to plan.

Roadblock: "Things always work out for me."

I love to hear this. These people already have a natural trust in life. The unfortunate part is that they may have a limited idea of how good life could be for them. I have two retired teachers in my life. I admire them both because they took early retirement and chose a life of adventure. They travelled abroad, were spiritual teachers at home, and inspired many people throughout their lives. As they reached their mid 60's, they were starting to see a fly in the ointment. With their ability to work dwindling, they were facing a life with much less money than they would like. Yes, they had food to eat and a roof over their heads, but not much more. After having lived such courageous lives, they are both facing the future with fear and dread. They cannot afford for anything to break down in their lives, including their health. Employers are not very forthcoming with high paying jobs for 65-year-old women who have been out of the workplace for the past 15 years. My friends failed to finance their life plan. They enjoyed the freedom of the present, but are now sacrificing that same freedom tomorrow. They failed to achieve a balance between security and freedom for today and tomorrow.

Roadblock: "God will take care of me."

To these people I respond: "Yes, and that is why he has put me in your path."

There is a story of a man full of faith. The radio blared news of a flood coming, but he took no notice of it. He had faith that God would save him. Neighbours came by and offered him a seat in their car as they were leaving. "No, thanks," the man replied. "God will save me." The water began to rise. As the water rose to his windowsills, a couple came by in a canoe and offered him a ride. "No, thanks," the man replied. "God will save me." The water continued to rise and the man perched on his rooftop. A helicopter flew overhead and wanted to throw him a line to safety. "No, thanks," the man replied. "I'm waiting for God to save me." The man drowned. Standing before God, the man cried and wept. "God, why did you forsake me? I had such great faith in you, but you let me die. Why?" In an exasperated voice, God said, "I did try to save you. I gave you notice on the radio. I had the neighbours offer you a ride. I sent the couple in the canoe. I even sent the helicopter, but you would not listen. Your arrogance cost you your life."

I believe that we come together, in whatever way, to give and receive from one another. We are meant to be a blessing to one another. Even though there were many challenges in taking this book from an idea to the final published edition, I always believed that continuing each step would bring me many gifts I could never have anticipated. And it has.

Now that you have this book in your hands, you have an opportunity to create what you have been longing for. As in the story of the drowned man, look at this book as your answer to being saved from a situation that does not create happiness for you.

Whether you are conscious of your life plan or not, you have one. Having no plan is also a plan. It is a plan to drift through life, pulled along by your subconscious mind. It can disguise itself as freedom, but the opposite is actually true. What is subconscious is out of your awareness and out of your control. As long as you are unaware of your plan, you literally have no power over it.

Often people are stuck making choices based on decisions they made about life so long ago that they no longer remember making them. Your past experiences and your parents' and ancestors' past experiences created your beliefs. You are making choices you are not conscious of. Sometimes those choices work for you and sometimes they don't. I'd like to help you clear up some of the decisions that are not working for you and build new beliefs and plans that will move you to where you would rather be, with greater ease and grace.

I can assure you that if you are not making new, conscious choices, you will keep repeating the same patterns over and over again until you do. You will continue to drive down the same road, travelling in circles, until you choose a new direction.

I once spent a short time with a man who was very clingy. He would constantly do things that pushed my buttons, and I would push him away. He would then whine and complain. He believed that his actions would bring me closer to him. His belief was so strong that he could not see the opposite results he was creating. Because he could not see it, he could do nothing about it. After many discussions, he still could not stop the behaviour. We eventually agreed to end the romantic side of our relationship. I love the way the cycle of life works. Even though he did not "get it" in our relationship, his next girlfriend behaved towards him as he did to me, and then, he got the lesson. He changed directions.

The universe places situations in front of us to help bring our subconscious to consciousness. The quicker we can become conscious, the easier our lives become. We may still hit the potholes of life, but they will not be so deep, they will not hurt as much, and the damage will be minimal. Eventually, we learn to how to drive around the potholes.

I'd like to bring some consciousness to your beliefs about your money and life situation. What are some of your earliest memories of money? What did they lead you to believe about money? About life?

_____

_____

_____

_____

_____

_____

_____

_____

_____

_____

_____

_____

_____

What money memories hold the strongest emotions for you? What emotions are they? What did these memories lead you to believe about money? About life?

_____

_____

_____

_____

_____

_____

_____

_____

_____

_____

_____

What did your mother (or other female figures) teach you about money? About life?

_____

_____

_____

_____

_____

_____

_____

_____
_____
_____
_____

What did your father (or other male figures) teach you about money? About life?

_____
_____
_____
_____
_____
_____
_____
_____
_____
_____
_____
_____

Looking at your overall experience of life, how have you been affected by your early memories and teachings?

_____
_____
_____
_____

_____

_____

_____

_____

_____

_____

_____

_____

Is there anything you would like to change your mind about, right now?

_____

_____

_____

_____

_____

_____

_____

_____

_____

Did you spend some time answering these questions? Did you dig deep within yourself? Did you fill in all the space provided? Did you learn anything? I have seen so many people read a planning book and then put it down in dismay because "it didn't work." I have found that it is often not the information that doesn't work, it is the reader who didn't make the effort to integrate the information. They didn't do their work.

I will give you lots of ideas about how to create your wildest dreams, but you have to do the inner research involved in the exercises. Just as you need to work your muscles to build strength, balance, and flexibility, you need to work your mind to harness its creative power. By exploring the depths of yourself and taking appropriate action, you will be able to change your world, one step at a time, on this journey. Try out each idea. If it doesn't seem to work for you, try the next idea. Each exercise is like a tool. Combined, they create a toolbox for the journey. There is a Tool Box at the end of this book for your reference.

If you would like to dig even deeper, try answering these questions while writing with your non-dominant hand.

Where will you be in five years, if you do not plan and decide on your destination?

_____

_____

_____

_____

_____

_____

_____

_____

_____

_____

_____

_____

_____

Where will you be in ten years, if you do not plan and decide on your destination?

_____

_____

_____

_____

_____

_____

_____

_____

_____

_____

Where do you want to be in ten years?

_____

_____

_____

_____

_____

_____

_____

_____

_____

_____

If you had only 24 hours to live, what would you most regret not saying, doing, seeing, or attempting? Who would you be with?

_____

_____

_____

_____

_____

_____

_____

_____

_____

_____

_____

_____

Considering the above, what changes do you want or need to make in the next seven days? Who do you need to contact? What do you need to say or do? Who can support you? Where is your peace? How can you increase your life energy?

_____

_____

_____

_____

_____

_____

_____

_____

_____

_____

_____

_____

_____

Over the next seven days, continue spending 15 minutes daily writing about your dream destination and how you could get there. Keep expanding your plans. As you look for new ideas, try this creative process. Close your eyes. Take ten slow, deep breaths and let yourself relax. Imagine that you are in the future, living your dream. Imagine that you are being interviewed about the steps you took to achieve this life. Listen to what you have to say. Have the interviewer ask any other questions that you want answered. Then write out what your future self has to say.

_____

_____

_____

_____

_____

_____

_____

_____

_____

_____

I know this last exercise may seem far-fetched for some of you, but unless you open to the idea of creative thinking, you are going to be putting in a lot of long hours and hard work. Think of labour as the masculine side of creation. It is pure muscle action. Think of creative thinking as the feminine side of creation. It is open and receptive to new ideas. It is beauty and grace. Both the masculine and feminine need to work together, in equal partnership, for the very best results. Feminine creative thinking opens to finding the best ideas and the masculine is then needed to put those ideas into action.

Affirmation: I choose to be happy. I choose my life.

WEEK 4
Your Road Log

Did you keep your commitment to yourself? Did you spend 15 minutes each day creating your happiness? If so, good for you! Were you tempted to miss a day? Is missing a day such a crime? No, but one day soon becomes, two, three, and ten and before you know it, you have abandoned your commitment. They say it only takes 21 days to create a new habit and if you have been committed, you are already two-thirds of the way there. However, if you missed even one day, you should start the count to 21, and the new, healthy habit, all over again.

It is easier to set a specific time each day for your daily exercise. Although I have outlined a structure that works for most people, use creative options to see how you can make it work in your world. For example, a couple had great success using this program. The wife read the book and did the program as I have structured it. Then, each night, she and her husband would walk by the river. She would ask him the same questions and then they would discuss both of their responses. Each day, they took at least 15 minutes to discuss the changes they wanted to create in their lives.

It's not important how you focus on your dreams, it is just important that you form a habit of doing so for a minimum of 15 minutes a day. If you are tempted to miss a day, ask yourself, "Is this reason, excuse, or activity more important than your happiness, your goals, or your reward for completing this program. If you choose to miss the day you have, in fact, answered yes to that question. Have the courage to face the truth. Make a conscious choice. It will save you a lot of frustration in the end. I am confident that as you progress, you will find that your day feels a little empty without taking those 15 minutes for yourself.

The most important thing is that you feel good about keeping your commitment to yourself. If writing every day starts to feel difficult or oppressive, ask yourself how you can make it fun. Use your creativity to find a way that works for you. This process is about learning from yourself, and if you (like me) tend to be a hard task master, it will soon lose its fun. When the fun goes, so does the inspiration, and soon it feels like a task or chore.

If time is your issue, write about that. If other people's needs are your issue, write about that. Write about how 15 minutes of focusing on yourself and your desires can be enjoyable. Would candles and soft music help? If you prefer to write in the evening, would a glass of wine make your writing more enjoyable? Make this practice as pleasurable as possible.

Never quit quitting, never stop starting

Whatever you do, just write. Even if you just pick up the pen and write, "I don't have time today." Keep doing that. Do whatever is possible.

I had my first cigarette at age five. When I see five-year-old little girls now, it doesn't seem possible! But by the time I was 12, I smoked regularly. At first I associated smoking with socializing and the thrill of rebellion. At 16, I smoked full-time. In my 20's and 30's, I smoked a minimum of 35 cigarettes a day. Later, I used smoking to calm myself. Then it became less socially acceptable and I started to quit. And I quit smoking over 200 times. Sometimes I quit every week.

Once, I quit for five years; another time for two years; other times, for a few hours. No matter how many times I failed, I kept on quitting.

The problem was that at the back of my mind, I was denying myself something that I believed I enjoyed. Then, when a weak moment appeared, (it always does) I started the cycle again. But I see repeatedly quitting smoking like adding a drop of food colouring to a pail of water. For a while, you won't notice the water change at all. Then, one day, with just one more drop of food colouring, the entire pail of water changes.

I believe I will never smoke again because I persisted and kept asking and wanting to quit. Eventually I made new associations with smoking. The last time I smoked, I chain-smoked all weekend with a dear friend who had just moved into a care home as she was developing dementia and memory loss. It was a sad, emotional time and I could see how smoking was helping keep our strong feelings in check. Soon after that, I spent some time with another friend who had just broken up with his wife and he smoked constantly. So again, I made a connection between emotional loss and smoking.

Now, I cannot stand the smell of people who smoke. It is interesting that while I still craved cigarettes and believed that I was missing something, I never once noticed how bad smokers smell. Now, I often find myself trapped in an elevator with someone who has just finished a cigarette. While it almost makes me gag, I am grateful because it is an ever present reminder of why I don't want to smoke. Something just happened one day—I changed my thoughts about smoking—and I no longer enjoyed my tobacco addiction. It's fascinating what finally inspires change.

The point of my smoking story is to both let you know that I know how difficult it can be to make positive changes and to inspire you to uphold your commitment to where you'd rather be in your life. If you stop writing, start again as soon as you can. If you can only write a sentence for today, commit to writing 15 minutes tomorrow. Keep on keeping on and you will get there. Remember that the more fun and enjoyable that you can make this daily reflection, the more likely you will stay focused. The more you focus, the faster you will achieve what you desire.

Take short trips first

With your list of wants and needs you have started to see new directions for your life and new ways to enjoy the journey. Has the scenery changed yet? Over the past three weeks, I know you have gained a lot of knowledge about what is most important to you. All knowledge, however, is useless unless you take action based on that knowledge: The benefits of that knowledge will then bear fruit.

New Knowledge + New Action = New Results

Choose one of your wants or needs that you think will be fairly easy to achieve. It's time to create concrete goals. Many teachers will ask you to choose the goal that is most important to you, but I have found that the one that is most important to me is often the biggest or hardest one to achieve. When we start with the hardest one, we risk disappointment and frustration, and then we are tempted to quit.

I'd like you to start with one of your easier goals so that you will have an opportunity to experience the process, gain faith in it, gain faith in yourself, and achieve success as soon as possible. Just like when you first learned to drive a car, you started with driving around the block before you set your sights on a cross-country tour. As always, you have choices. You can choose any goal that you desire. Perhaps you want to sign up for a class, start exercising, or purchase something that you actually have the cash for.

The goal is _____

Look a little deeper. Perhaps your goal is a means to an even greater end. Start with your goal and then complete the same sentence five times. For example, when I did this exercise, it looked like this: If I had $10 million dollars, then I'd feel financially secure. If I had $10 million dollars, then I could support children in Africa. If I had $10 million dollars, then I would only work part-time. If I had $10 million dollars, then I would live part of the year in Mexico. If I had $10 million dollars, I would be able to give more workshops.

For me, this goal seems to be more about the ability to give more of my time and money, than actual money accumulation. Finding the deeper desire will save you a lot of time and energy. Using my example, I could have put a lot of attention on accumulating cash, but it would not be satisfying to me because I would not achieve what I truly want. As this process brought greater clarity about what was truly important to me, I saw that I could give more of my time and money without having $10 million dollars. Now you try it.

If I had/become/achieve _____ (the goal), then I'd _____.

If I had/become/achieve _____ (the goal), then I'd _____.

If I had/become/achieve _____ (the goal), then I'd _____.

If I had/become/achieve _____(the goal), then I'd _____.

If I had/become/achieve _____(the goal), then I'd _____.

What is your true goal? _____

You could achieve this by:

_____

_____

_____

_____

_____

_____

_____

_____

_____

_____

_____

_____

_____

Now, ask yourself which action feels like the best direction to go in or the best place to start. Within the next seven days, take that step.

Sometimes it will get you to your destination in one giant step. Sometimes a step will only get you partway towards your goal. If so, make another list of possible actions, choose the one that feels most appropriate to you, and take that step. Then choose the next action that will enhance your life, and so the process continues.

Stops along the way

Let's talk a little more about goals and goal setting. A few pointers may be helpful. First of all, the above process is basic, but can be very helpful in achieving shorter term goals. If you are a procrastinator, you must master this step before you can truly move on. If you are an achiever, take care not to hurt yourself by trying to achieve all 150 wants and needs this week.

In many goal setting programs, the facilitators talk about the importance of adding dates for the accomplishment of your goals. Personally, I have mixed thoughts about creating deadlines for my goals. I believe that procrastinators must have not only a completion date, but also several smaller completion dates along the way—although a procrastinator could also use a completion date to delay starting! Achievers can benefit from completion dates so that they do not push themselves too hard, but they more often use completion dates to push themselves into stressful and unbalanced lives.

Benefits of Goal Dating:
- can keep you focused
- can prompt you to action
- can keep you moving when tempted to stop
- can give you a finish line—a celebration point!
- can ensure that you accomplish the goal

Weakness of Goal Dating:

> - can be used as an excuse to quit, if you miss the date
> - can be used to circumvent personal intuition
> - can be used to create a feeling of failure
> - can push you past a healthy effort
> - can persuade you to delay starting
> - can tempt you to stray from personal integrity just to meet the goal deadline

When a goal proves a little more challenging than I would like, I ask myself: "How can I do this and still have fun?" It really helps to try to reinterpret the feelings of hard work you have toward your goal into something you find enjoyable. The question helps me become more creative. When I start to get nervous just before a workshop or talk, I repeat this little ditty: "My nervousness gave way when I started to play." It is not poetry, but I came up with it through an inspiration process, and it works for me.

At my worst, I can be a workaholic and a perfectionist. Does that make a perfect workaholic? To remind myself to relax, I ask myself "Where's the beach?" It is a powerful statement because being near water soothes my soul. I really remember and trust that everything is going to work out perfectly. The word "beach" is an image that gets my senses immediately involved—I see the water and feel the breeze on my skin. An attitude of playfulness always strengthens my ability to open to inspiration. Once I'm inspired, it no longer feels like work!

How do you balance work and play? How do you relax when you are feeling stressed? And, how do you get motivated when you feel lethargic?

_____

_____

_____

_____

_____

_____

_____

_____

_____

_____

_____

Write a sentence that will help bring you back into balance.

_____

_____

_____

_____

_____

What Your Desire Looks Like

The other thing to keep in mind is that the achievement of your goal may not look like you thought it would. For example, I once wrote down a desire to have a personal hug from Dr. Leo Buscaglia. He was a well-known professor and speaker who always gave any audience member who wanted one a hug at the end of his presentation. Not knowing how to get a hold of his speaking schedule (a time before the Internet), I wrote to him in care of his book publisher. I fully expected to get a note from a secretary or other administrative person. Imagine my surprise and delight, when I received a letter, personal and direct, from Leo himself. Although he was on a break from his speaking tour, I know that I did, in fact, achieve my goal—a personal hug from Leo. It was not as I had envisioned it, but it was so much more. His letter is framed and hangs in my office to this day. Be open to having your dreams unfold in a similar way—not as you had envisioned but better!

One of the things that I love about getting to know the expatriates who have chosen to live in Puerto Vallarta, is that they are "outside the box" thinkers. They have generated amazing experiences. They are highly creative, and have usually been hugely successful in their fields. They are business people, recording artists, painters, musicians, dancers, surfers, and homemakers. One friend is a lawyer who made her fortune by opening wedding chapels. Another started doing business in Asia over 30 years ago. Another has a platinum album. Others have lived on boats and travelled around the world. They are people with fascinating stories who continually inspire me to open my mind to greater possibilities for my life.

Monica's story is filled with examples from the Principles of Creation. If you are following my suggested program, you will have a list of the Principles on your mirror. You can also refer to the Introduction if you require a short refresher course. Once you read Monica's story, go back and see which Principles she incorporated in her journey to where she wanted to be. Monica was born in Warsaw, Poland, during the communist regime. Her memory of being ten years old and waiting in line for an hour and a half to buy a jar of jelly and a jar of mayonnaise brought tears to my eyes. At the time, Poland was feeding Russia and had very little left over. The jars of jelly and mayonnaise were such a treat for the whole family. Even though her father was an electrical engineer and her mother a principal at the school, they only made the equivalent of about $20 a month. As she was coming home on the bus, alone, a fellow passenger ran into her. She fell and the jars broke. So did her heart. She decided that this was not how she wanted to live her life. At 16, she knew that she wanted to go to the US, so she started to take English classes and prepare herself. One year her break came when she found out that a cousin was leaving a nanny's position in the States and offered it to Monica. Monica could go to the US for three months—she was ready and leapt at the opportunity. Once in the United States, she didn't want to return to Poland and lived illegally for several years. During that time, America was offering lotteries for immigration. Monica entered herself, her mother, her father, and her sister. Her mother won the lottery and the whole family got to legally immigrate to New York. Because Monica was over 21, she was not included.

Can you imagine how she felt? She was happy for her family and yet sad for herself. It must have been a very confusing time for her. The administration then offered all illegal residents the opportunity to return home and then re-enter the US as legal residents. Monica leapt at the chance to make things right. After returning to Poland, she was immediately denied a visa to return. But, there was no stopping Monica. She went and fought for the visa—and won! After being back and forth between the two countries a couple of times, Monica recently became an American citizen.

At the age of ten, Monica started to form a desire. At 16, she made a decision. At 18, she took a leap. Faced with opportunities and setbacks, she was committed to her dream. At 35, she had achieved her dream of US citizenship. Achieving her dream took some time, but she will tell you it was worth it. At age 35, 80 % of the children she went to school with are still living in Warsaw in relative poverty. They just made different choices.

Your challenge this week is to:

1. Take at least one step toward one of your goals. If you would like to take more steps toward achieving more goals, feel free to do so.

2. Choose your top ten most important goals. These will be goals that you have a burning desire for, or that challenge you the most. Choose the goals with the most emotional attachment for you. If fear shows up around one of them, write and explore that fear this week. What about it scares you? Are you afraid of something that you have associated with the goal? For example, I had a block around relationships that was related to my fear of conflict. Identify what truly needs to be cleared up so that you can achieve this burning desire. Again, try to see what desire is under the goal. What do you think you will have once you achieve that goal? Perhaps there is an easier way to achieve the deeper desire, right now.

3. Write out your top ten goals in positive, emotional, powerful present tense sentences, during your 15 minutes of daily reflection in your Road Log this week. Make them into affirmations. For example, when I wanted to earn $100,000, I wrote: "I am having fun, living in peace, and making at least $100,000 per year." The "I am" is present tense. "Having fun and living in peace" creates a feeling. $100,000 is the goal. The sentence makes me feel good. It raises my energetic vibration. The belief under the sentence was that with an income of $100,000 I would be having fun and living in peace. I realized that belief was faulty. The deeper goals are fun and peace, and I don't need the money for that. As you dig deeper into your goals, you will find your ultimate desires. Remember that if you do not take the time to find those deeper and more meaningful goals, you will become a taskmaster and then eventually become disillusioned and disappointed because your achievements will not feel satisfying to you.

From now on, always write your desires out as affirmations. Although you wrote out "I want" and "I need," those methods were to help you feel comfortable with getting to know your desires. Do not create more wants or needs. Instead, bring that desire into your current experience of life. Words have power and whatever we say remains our experience. So if we continued to say "I want," we would continue to want indefinitely. If we say "I have" or "I am" we create the experience of actually having it. Remember that what we focus on expands, so focus on having instead of wanting.

Do you feel comfortable making a statement that you know is not true today? If you have a strong internal "no" to such a statement, adjust it slightly by using the word "open." "I am open to having fun, living in peace, and making at least

$100,000 per year." If you still hear an internal "no" to this, it is time to do some digging into why you're not open. Begin by writing out questions to yourself and trust your answers. Ask: "Why am I not open?" Keep questioning and answering until you find peace with your goal.

Affirmation: I choose to be happy!
I am open to receive all that is good.

WEEK 5
Detours

Wow! Things are moving forward and if you have kept to your daily practice of writing 15 minutes a day, you have already instilled one great habit that can serve you for the rest of your life. Taking time for yourself is not a luxury, it is a necessity. Stick to it.

What has been your greatest discovery over the past few weeks?

_____

_____

_____

_____

_____

_____

_____

_____

_____

_____

_____

_____

Simple as these exercises may appear, this is not an easy program. As you progress day after day, you will hit many roadblocks or places where you will be tempted to quit. I have encountered many teachers who told me that if I followed their rules, my life would get much easier. While each field of study opened new doors for me and made important improvements in parts of my life, I still had disappointments. With each disappointment came disillusionment and a temptation to quit. Life is a journey, and as we take each new step, a greater challenge will be put in our path. This is the journey of life. It's an evolutionary process that keeps us learning and growing.

There are always points where choices are made. The question is: "Am I willing to be bigger?" By "bigger" I mean choosing to have more in our lives, to live in a bigger way, to truly expand our consciousness and our lives. Workshop leader and author, Chuck Spezzano told me that pain is inevitable, but suffering is optional. I have found that while choosing to expand may bring us growing pains, choosing to stay stuck is a choice to suffer.

By now, you have probably been tempted to miss a day of your Road Log or not answer some of my questions. Life happens. I am not saying it is OK to miss a day, but I want to acknowledge that temptations and distractions surround us. They may look as though they're coming from others, but really they come from ourselves. I believe the best way to deal with our distractions and temptations is to study them and make a game plan about how to handle them if and when they show up along the way to where you'd rather be.

Roadblock: "I'm happy as I am"

Once in while, I hear people say "I am happy as I am" or "I am happy enough." While "I'm happy as I am" sounds like a desirable destination, it is really meant as a resting place.

We all need rest, but too much of a good thing can leave you stuck. I am not asking you to be perfect, just to be dedicated to your needs and desires. If you hit this roadblock, ask yourself, "Am I tempted to rest, or quit, because I feel happy or because I feel frustrated?"

For those encountering this roadblock, my sense is that you don't want to deal with whatever is in front of you—you are afraid of opening a can of worms. It often seems like too much work. Why is it so hard (in a culture full of so much) to create true happiness? I believe that it is because we have broken hearts. We have given up because of painful losses or disappointments in the past. We settle for what is right in front of us, instead of going for what really matters. We try to be OK with something that is not right for us. We lower our expectations of life and seldom try again.

Change can be messy. Just look at what happens when you clean out your closet. It looks far worse in the middle of the project than before you began. It is often not until you finish that you can see the benefits of ever starting to reorganize. That is why it is so important to begin with the end in mind. That is why you constantly ask, "What do I want?" Knowing where you are going, and what the rewards are, makes the messiness worthwhile.

"I'm happy as I am" is the favourite saying of an inner character called "the rebel." While the word "rebel" may bring up stereotypes of men on motorcycles, you each have your own inner rebel. He is the one who doesn't want to be told what to do. We all rebel against being told what to do, even if it comes out in passive ways. That is one of the reasons I ask you to find out what *you* want to do. You must become your own authority.

We also have inner ideas that contradict each other. In effect, we are rebelling against ourselves. Parts of us want to move forward, while parts of us are afraid to change. Consider dialoguing with each of these parts. I address this more deeply later in the book, but for now, if you are tempted to stop writing each day, choose to write from the part of yourself that doesn't want to change, that doesn't want to go towards what your heart is calling for. Give a voice to your rebel and he will become your freedom rider.

Now, there are many moments in my life when I am so fulfilled that I can't think of any way I could be happier. These are the moments when I have reached my current destination. I have reached the limits of my current thinking. These are moments to be celebrated and savoured. And then, a little while later, I think: "What's next?"

There is always more to be done, seen, experienced, and contributed. Sometimes, people will try to hang on to the wonderful feeling of the moment by not wanting to make any changes. They think: "If it's not broke, don't fix it." This can be a fear of change. I have found that you can take that feeling of celebration with you, but if you become attached to it, it begins to fade.

There is no such thing as stopping. We are either moving forward, or we are dying. Just like the cycle of birth and death, the natural order of life, we are either moving in a life direction or a death direction. Watching what happens to people when they retire is very illuminating. If they leave work to start a new adventure, they are full of life. As soon as they stop expanding their experiences, they start to slow down, shrivel, and eventually die. You can see how contraction happens in your muscles and you can see it working in your brain, and you can see it working in your life. Don't stop living. Don't settle for how things are. Even if everything is already wonderful, it can be even more wonder-full.

The 21 Day Program

Just as choosing premium fuel enhances your car's performance, so does putting energy into your desires. Notice that I said energy, not work. There is a huge difference here. Far too many people increase their labour, but never truly achieve their wildest dreams because you can only work to the level of physical exhaustion. Working to that level throws your life out of balance and creates far more problems or distractions from your goal, both physical and emotional. People can end up working against themselves.

So, how do you increase the energy for your desire? I work with my version of the 21 Day Program, first introduced to me by Bob Proctor, a noted motivational speaker and author. For 21 days, for a minimum of 15 minutes per day, visualize and start writing about what it would be like to have your wildest dreams come true. As I have mentioned, I create clarity when I put pen to paper. Once I start to write, it is easier for me to visualize. Some people have an easier time changing the order by visualizing and then writing.

Let's start with your top ten most important wants, needs, goals, or affirmations. Through writing them out in strong, emotional statements over the past weeks, they have grown in vision and clarity. **The next step is for you to write those top ten out as a story—the desired story of your life—your destination.** Write the story in so much detail that you can see it, taste it, smell it, hear it, and feel it. Ensure that all senses are included in your story.

For example, if your goal is to have a certain amount of money, how will your life be different when you have that amount? Where will you live? What will you be doing? Who will you be doing it with? What will your food taste like?

What will your home smell like? What colours will surround you? Can you hear laughter around you? Are the birds singing? How do you feel?

Start writing a story about having your desires. Make it as detailed as possible. Ensure that you have a lot of emotion in your vision. Emotion increases the vibration of your dream. As that vibration increases, it increases the strength of the results that are magnetized into your life. The Dream has more Power.

Scientists have proven that everything is energy in motion. This energy in motion is called vibration. The better we feel, the higher our own vibration. Think about when you start a new relationship. You feel loved and good about yourself and that person. You have all kinds of energy to stay up half the night and still bounce into work. Your vibration is high. Furthermore, the sun seems to shine brighter, the birds seem to sing sweeter, and nothing much really bothers you. Ever notice how many good things happen to you when you first fall in love?

Contrast that with being dumped. You don't feel loved. Many hours are spent rehashing where things went wrong. Either you or your former lover is to blame. This is a much lower vibration. It becomes harder to get up in the morning. And when you do it's probably raining and someone will be angry. So, therefore, what you think about a situation determines how you feel and the energetic vibration you emit. The energetic vibration acts as a magnet to attract more of things that are at the same vibration. The happier you are, the more you will attract things, people, and events that you enjoy. Also, when you are happy, you choose to see the good in everything. When you are unhappy you are also busy attracting like things to the feeling or vibration you are holding. So if you are angry, things will continue to happen that build on that anger. You will then choose to see the negative in everything. For a deeper study of this concept, I would recommend *Ask and It is Given* by Esther and Jerry Hicks.

For example, let's say you want a new car for your journey. If you start focusing on having a new car, your experience will be flooded with options—blue, red, green, automatic, five-speed, fully loaded, or bare basics. Now, if you focus on the details of what you want, you build the picture, and begin to imagine what it feels like to have that specific car. You may see yourself speeding down the country road in your shiny, hot, red Mazda 626, five-speed, fully loaded with heated seats. Your love is by your side, the wind is blowing through your hair, and you are laughing and enjoying all the fun you have together. As you add more details to the picture, you will increase your ability to attract (magnetize) your dream, because you are creating more emotion. With the power of your emotional picture, you are planting the seeds of creation in your subconscious mind, re-writing your script of possibilities.

Here's how we all continue to create our lives. For most of us, the process happens automatically:

Your Past Experiences
Create
Your Memories and Imprints on the Mind
Which Create
Your Beliefs
Which Create
Your Daily Thoughts
Which Create
Your Feelings and Energetic Vibration
That Create
Your Choices
And Create
Your Actions
And Create
Your Results
That Create
Your Past Experiences

And it keeps continuing and reinforcing all you believe and do.

This is the process that keeps recreating the same old stuff. Some of it we like, but some of it we don't. Luckily, we can change our results by changing the imprints on our subconscious minds. Through the visualization process, we are actually creating new "memories." The mind does not differentiate between what is real and what is imagined! Once we implant a strong enough vision, we begin automatically to create new beliefs, actions, and results. This is conscious creation. Many of the great professional athletes use this powerful process. They enhance their performance and results by repeatedly imagining the results they want to create. The basketball player sees the ball going through the hoop hundreds of times before it really does. The runner sees himself crossing the finish line first. The hockey player sees the puck entering the net. People making millions of dollars a year use visualization.

You can also reframe your past experiences so that you think and feel very differently about them. As your thoughts and feelings change, so do your results. I will say more about that later, but for now let's work on implanting the seeds for the greatest life you can imagine.

If you get stuck writing, put down your pen, close your eyes, and start to envision scenes of what it would be like. You could also pretend that you are talking to a friend and telling them about how your life is once you have achieved your top ten. Remember to write your story in positive, present tense using emotional words. Involve every one of your senses. Do whatever it takes to completely fill in every line provided for you to write in.

The Destination

_____
_____
_____
_____
_____
_____
_____
_____

_____

_____

_____

_____

_____

_____

_____

_____

_____

Congratulations! I know that took some creative thinking and some very big stretches. **For the next seven days, spend ten minutes each day visualizing your dream destination.** Close your eyes and play your story like a movie in your mind. You will also find that as the days go by, you will create an even bigger version of your dream. Let the story grow and expand. Go with it! Dare to dream big. Have the courage to reach for a fantasy. In this process, you are opening to listen to your heart's desires. Do not limit yourself. Let it flow. Do not let your personal beliefs or limitations stop you. Let the dream build itself. You are learning to listen to your heart and it has bigger dreams and destinations for you than you are currently able to imagine.

Spend the remaining five minutes per day writing out the newest version of your vision. If this is hard for you, reverse the process and write out the dream, letting new thoughts and ideas come in. Then spend five minutes visualizing what you have written. It is said that it takes 21 days to create a new habit. We want to create a new habit of consciously creating your life. **For the next 21 days stay focused on seeing yourself living the dream.** Write out your vision in present moment terms: I have, I see, I am doing, I hear, I experience, I feel. With the 21 Day Process, you are building energy in your desire. You are bringing it into the present moment.

This book is a direct result of the power of the 21 Day Process. When I first thought about writing a book, I assumed that I would do it far in the future, perhaps five years down the road. By the end of the 21 Day Process, I had committed to go to Mexico to start the book the following year. The 21 Day Process had moved the accomplishment of my vision from five years to six months! I had never written a book before and I certainly did not know how I was going to find the money to take a month off work. Where was I going to stay? What about my dog and my house? All the details could have stopped me, but I did not let that happen. Even at the end of January, a friend asked me what I was going to do as I had not yet acquired the finances to go to Mexico for a month. I informed her that quitting was not an option. I was committed to going. I could see writing the book, and nothing else. I went to a few courses on publishing and was told that it would cost about $20,000 to publish my book. I had no idea where the money would come from and then I won the "Write Stuff" publishing contract. I know this was the Principles of Creation in action. Sometimes we are given the whole road map, and sometimes we can only see the next step. As I completed the only step I could see, the next step was promptly delivered. This is the power of the 21 Day Process, the power of commitment to living my dream. And if I can do it, so can you!

Affirmation: I am open to having all of my dreams come true!

WEEK 6
Flat Tires

Every problem is a fear of, and a refusal to,
change, to take a new way, become a leader.
— Chuck Spezzano, Ph.D., author and workshop facilitator

Welcome back. I hope that you are proud of yourself. You are moving. You have started to turn the car around and head in the direction of your heart. This week we are going to look at another belief that can deflate you tires: "Change is too much work!"

Would you stop to fix a flat tire, or continue to drive? Yes, it is work to fix it, but it is far more work and more expensive later if you continue to drive on the flat tire. You could lose the tire, the rim, your alignment, your whole car, and if there were an accident because of it, you could lose your life. Life works the same way. Eventually something feels flat in your life or out of balance. If you ignore it long enough, it can cost you a life of fulfillment.

I was married to a man who constantly longed to travel from place to place. He claimed that my need to settle down was holding him back. I looked at my desires and knew that I wanted him in my life but I also wanted a form of security. My solution was to save up for "the journey." I wanted a new truck and trailer to live in during our travels, and $25,000 in savings for our return. He agreed. I thought that we had arrived at a win/win solution. The next thing I knew, he wanted to buy something extravagant. I discussed the need to save for our journey. He replied that the journey was not important enough to him to save for. Here I had been beating myself up about my need for security and had searched my soul for a way to create a way to make his dream come true! And in the end, he didn't really want to make the choices to attain what he had said he wanted.

I have seen this far too often. People make themselves and others miserable by complaining about not having something, but are unwilling to do anything about making it happen. This tendency to moan is about choice. Either truly choose to have what you say you want, or let it go. Don't live a lie!

Yes, it does take effort to change your life, but it also takes effort to live a miserable life. How much energy does it take to fret over your bills, or live in fear of your future? How much work is it to stay in a miserable relationship or a boring career? Think about it. It takes more effort to live an unfulfilled life than a passionate and meaningful life. The choice is yours.

With this program it takes only 15 minutes of internal effort a day to change your life. Tell the truth to yourself. Whenever you are tempted to give up on a goal, ask yourself the following questions. If any part of this program feels like too much work, ask yourself:

What do I say I want?

_____

_____

_____

_____

_____

_____

_____

_____

_____

Why am I afraid of having it? (Yes, there is something you are avoiding, or you would already have it in your life.)

_____

_____

_____

_____

_____

_____

_____

_____

_____

What will I have to do to get it?

_____

_____

_____

_____

_____

_____

_____

How can I reduce my work load or have fun achieving it all?

_____

_____

_____

_____

_____

_____

_____

_____

_____

_____

How will I feel when I have my goal?

_____

_____

_____

_____

_____

_____

_____

_____

_____

How will I feel if I don't go after it?

_____

_____

_____

_____

_____

_____

_____

_____

_____

_____

Is it worth going after? Yes or No

Either get moving, or let it go!

Install the GPS: Your Internal Guidance System

Following your Road Map takes integrity. I offer suggestions that I believe will best serve you, but don't make me your authority. You are the authority in your life. Listen to yourself. If you get nothing else out of this book but the ability to hear yourself, your own inner voice, then it will have been well worth the investment. If something I say doesn't feel true to you, don't just accept it. Check it out. Try it out. Investigate and draw your own conclusion. Everything is up to you. You always have choices. What do you want?

To possess integrity, we must be able to say both yes and no with equal ease. Many people have developed the social grace of saying yes, but meaning no. No wonder we have communication problems! It's cruel to make people wait to hear from someone who said they'd call or wait for them to do something they said they would do. It is equally dreadful if you are busy with activities, organizations, and people you aren't really interested in. People who can only say yes have a huge need for acceptance from others. Having the courage to say no and still keep the lines of communication open, builds intimacy, solves issues, and builds trust.

On the other side are those who can only say "no." Afraid of losing their personal power, they can't seem to cooperate with others. One of my teachers, Henri McKinnon, says: "Rebels are leaders who have lost their confidence." I'm talking about this early in the book because you must be able to hear your own truth about what you are committed to achieving in your life. Some goals might sound good to you, but are you saying yes on the inside, as well as the outside? Knowing your honest answer comes from listening to your feelings. Does the goal fill you with excitement? Do you feel discomfort or fear?

Crossroads: Different Directions

If you outwardly (consciously) want to pursue a goal but are inwardly (unconsciously) saying no, your efforts will reap few results. You are fighting yourself. Take the time to investigate the conflicts in your desires. In my journal, I write from the side of me that is saying no and I then write from the side of me that is saying yes. Just like in any relationship, I continue to communicate between both sides until there is unity or peace and until I'm 100% committed to heading in a single direction.

Think of a goal, want, need, or affirmation that you have mixed feelings about. If you think there isn't one, review your lists. Pick one that seems too big, too extravagant, or too outrageous. Your dreams should be challenging, exciting, and even a little scary. What dream have you been avoiding?

_____

_____

_____

_____

_____

_____

_____

What do you like about it?

_____

_____

_____

_____

_____

_____

_____

What is making you uncomfortable about it?

_____

_____

_____

_____

_____

_____

_____

_____

Write from the side of you that is against the dream, to the side that wants it. Why don't you want it? What scares you? Why are you feeling uncomfortable?

_____

_____

_____

_____

_____

_____

_____

_____

_____

_____

_____

_____

Now try communicating from the side of you that wants this dream, to the side that doesn't want the dream. Why do you want it? How will it enhance your life? How will you feel when you have this goal?

_____

_____

_____

_____

_____

_____

_____

_____

_____

_____

_____

Continue writing from each side until both sides can reach a mutually agreeable decision. If you are ever in conflict with another person, try taking on each other's point of view. Once you argue their side, and they argue yours, there is much greater understanding and clarity. This usually ends the conflict very quickly.

Integration Process for Dilemmas and Conflicts (Finding Energetic Balance)

This is a great exercise to use when working with dilemmas and conflicting beliefs, with others or within yourself. I find it very helpful to prepare for any communication that might need resolution. Close your eyes. Take ten slow, deep breaths. Imagine that you are connected to the universe with a band of white light. Now imagine that you are also connected to the Earth energetically. Imagine and feel the energy coming up through the soles of your feet, your legs, filling your body, arms, and head. Then "see" the energy leaving through the top of your head. Now reverse that and see the Universal energy coming into the top of your head, travel through and fill your body, and exit out the bottom of your feet. Think about the situation that is concerning you. Ask to be brought to your centre and feel balanced. Move your hands approximately three feet apart. Turn your palms up. Imagine one side of the dilemma or conflict as a ball (of energy) in your left hand. What colour is it? Feel the weight of it. Now imagine putting the other side of the dilemma or conflict in your right hand. Again, imagine it as a ball. What colour is this ball? Feel the weight of it. Compare how the weight feels to the other ball in your left hand. With the balls still attached to your hands, turn your palms so that they face each other. Slowly begin to move your hands together. Think of the question you are looking to answer. Be open to hear any internal messages as you do this. Keep in touch with the feeling of energy in each palm. Do you feel any resistance between the two hands as you slowly bring them together? Gently integrate the energy of both sides as you clasp your hands together. Now that the energies have been brought together, bring your hands to your heart chakra. Relax and breathe. Be willing to find the true answers that will bring you balance. If you have not received a better resolution during this process, watch for it in your thoughts over the next few days. It will come.

Be Your Own Cheerleader

Does your current vision of yourself permit you to be who you want to be and have what you want to have? For example, if you see yourself as weak, it is very hard to feel good about entering an Ironman contest. It is hard to enter a drag race when you see yourself riding a scooter. Who do you see yourself as, in relation to your aspirations? For example: If you want to be a millionaire, do you have the skills to manage that much money?

_____

_____

_____

_____

_____

_____

_____

_____

_____

_____

Does your current self-talk (what you say to yourself about yourself) build you up or tear you down? Does it support your dreams or shred your confidence?

_____

_____

_____

_____

_____

_____

_____

_____

_____

_____

Do you reward yourself—not just for what you do, but also for who you are? While we often crave acknowledgement and love from others, it is what we tell ourselves that creates our truth. I have found that even a few kind and supportive words, said to myself, are a real reward. Becoming my own cheerleader has opened the door for others to champion me as well. Remember that the way others treat us is a reflection of how we are treating ourselves.

Stand in front of a mirror. Look into your eyes. Tell yourself what you appreciate about yourself—out loud. Take your time. Let each self appreciation sink in. At a minimum, say four or five things that you appreciate about yourself. End with telling yourself "I love you." It is a lovely way to start or finish your day. Start seeing the effects reflected back to you in your life.

Also pay attention to the things that you say to and about yourself throughout the day. Are you increasing or lowering your vibration? What about treating yourself to little gifts?

If you only reward yourself for doing well, you are building a foundation for "conditional love." This is where we only give love and acknowledgement for achieving and doing. It creates a do-do-doer. Perhaps you know of a few workaholics. Perhaps you are one. Conditional love creates the belief that you are only worthy of love, if you are achieving. That continues into the belief that "if I fail or rest, I am no longer loveable." Give yourself love and rewards for who you are. Give to yourself each and every day!

Now, if you are finding places where you don't believe that it is possible for you to have the life you are dreaming of, brainstorm ten possible strategies to help narrow the gap between where you are and where you want to be. For example, if you want to be a millionaire you could:

• Read about millionaires and emulate them.
• Learn about money—making it and managing it.
• Dress for success.
• Find places to socialize with people with money.

What's your list?

_____

_____

_____

_____

_____

_____

_____

_____

_____

_____

_____

_____

How do you feel about it now?

_____

_____

_____

_____

Do you feel empowered? Do you expect success with your goal? _____

If you do not expect success, it is very unlikely that you will achieve it. Keep working with your visualization until you can see, feel, hear, and taste success.

You can repeat this process until you feel peaceful about either going forward or letting go of the goal. You can do that now, or set a date to come back to it. If you are going to move forward with the goal, really look at your expectations. Are you going to just try? Trying hides a place where there is doubt in your ability to succeed in this endeavour. Once you expect success, it is yours!

Here are four things you can do with any goal:
• Do it
• Dump it
• Date it
• Delegate it

Just don't sit on the fence about it. Sitting on the fence means there is a conflict and it will rob your energy until you reach a decision and feel complete with it.

For the next seven days, continue writing in your journal for 15 minutes a day and visualize your dream destination—the fabulous place you'd rather be. Remember that if you miss a day during the 21 days, you need to start again. Like last week, spend ten minutes visualizing and five minutes writing about your vision of heaven on earth. Or vice versa. If there are any goals within your vision that you do not 100% desire, go back to the crossroads, the places where your mind is split, and once more go through this week's exercises to heal conflicts in your mind.

NOTE: For next week's exercise you will need a piece of Bristol board, a pair of scissors, a glue stick and a variety of magazines.

Affirmation: I choose to be happy! I am clear where I am going and what's right for me.

WEEK 7
Plot Your Route

You are in the home stretch of the 21 Day Process of building your dream. As with any new destination, it is helpful to plot your route on a road map. It is good to see where you are going and to highlight the roads you want to travel. Then you are less distracted by the multiple choices that are available. This week we are going to have some fun and call on another form of your creativity. You are going to build a collage—a picture of your desired objective. Some people call it a "Dream Board."

Go through the magazines you have. In the magazines, find pictures and words that convey the essence of your dream. Cut them out and start building a possible layout on your board. Don't start gluing things down until you have finalized the board layout. If you have artistic talents, you can also include some of your own drawings of the dream. One of my workshop attendees used Photoshop to put their own face on the pictures they chose for their board.

If you really love what you create, have it dry mounted. Dry mounting is relatively inexpensive and will keep your Dream Board in excellent condition. Whether you have it professionally framed, or just use tape, hang your board somewhere you will see it every day.

I love this week's assignment. I often do a new Dream Board each January 1st. If you enjoy the process, try sharing it with your friends and family. It can be a fun, beautiful, intuitive, and highly creative thing to do. Then, throughout the year, watch as the pictures and words show up as reality in your life. I keep a few years at a time as they are also a very good image of my life journey. My very first one was done on a brown background. The pictures were dark and had very little colour. A few years later, the background was hot pink and the pictures bounced off the page. I could see that each board was a great reflection of where I was at the time.

That's it for this week. **During the next seven days, continue with ten minutes of visualizing your top ten goals as a story and five minutes of writing about your visualization, or vice versa.** Complete your collage. If you feel the urge to journal about other issues, please do so as an addition to the 15 minutes you spend on your dreams.

Affirmation: I choose to be happy.
I create with fun and enthusiasm.

WEEK 8
Clear Travel Plans

Congratulations! You have successfully completed the 21 Day Process. The seeds of your dreams are now firmly planted and fertilized within your subconscious mind. Take a few moments to describe your dream in one sentence.

_____

_____

_____

_____

You can use this sentence as your affirmation. Stick it on your bathroom mirror or find little ways to remind yourself each day. I use small stickers. I put them throughout my house and office and whenever I see the sticker, it reminds me to say my dream affirmation. I know of a successful man who chooses an object that reminds him of the goal and then carries that object in his pocket. Each time he feels the object, it brings his dream to mind. Be creative and enjoy the process.

Even without conscious thought, you will continue to see progress towards your heart's desire. It may not be this month, this year, or next, but I assure you that when you look back in a few years from now, you will be able to see that your dream is in the process of coming true. Fifteen years ago, I did the 21 Day Process towards the dream of becoming a workshop leader and facilitator. Throughout the years, I have actually tried to throw that dream away. I have even consciously changed my mind, but the dream persists. You have the power to stop your dream, but from now on, your dream will keep knocking at your door, waiting for you to open the door again.

But, having just completed the 21 Day Process, I am sure that you are still committed to achieving your dream. You can accelerate that achievement by working with the shorter term goals you wrote about earlier, which will move you closer to your dream. Your dream may be to travel the world. An example of a short-term goal is to learn to speak another language, or start a savings program, or read books, or do research on the Internet. It's a good idea to once again ask and answer the questions from Week 4.

Just spend a few minutes envisioning your dream. Have it firmly planted in your conscious and subconscious mind. Then quietly ask yourself:

What is the goal:_____

Now complete these sentences:
If I had/become/achieve _____(the goal), then I'd_____
If I had/become/achieve _____(the goal), then I'd _____.
If I had/become/achieve _____(the goal), then I'd _____.
If I had/become/achieve _____(the goal), then I'd _____.
If I had/become/achieve _____(the goal), then I'd _____.

What is the deeper goal? _____

I could achieve this by:

_____

_____

_____

_____

_____

_____

_____

_____

_____

_____

Did you include any ways to have fun? Now, ask yourself which action feels like the best direction to go in. What has the most positive energy? Which feels the most exciting? Begin immediately.

Enjoy the Journey

Now that you know where you want to go, let's spend a few minutes deciding what kind of trip it is going to be. After all, what is the point of getting out of bed if you're not going to have a good time? Balancing fun and focus is important. It is like balancing your inner truck driver, who goes from point A to point B and is focused on work, and your inner Sunday driver, who stops at every point of interest, but ends up back where he started, with no purpose but enjoyment and passing time. I am not talking about indulging in fun as a distraction from your goals, but about using fun as a driving principle. When you are focusing on your goals, always ask, "How can I do this and have fun?" When you are having fun, you are inspired and full of energy. Work feels like fun and fun is full of purpose. You will arrive ahead of schedule and feel refreshed!

When do you feel the happiest?

_____

_____

_____

_____

With your current dream in mind:

What do you need to enjoy the journey to your dream?

_____

_____

_____

_____

How can you increase the experience of joy along the way?

_____

_____

_____

_____

When and how will you rest? Celebrate?

_____

_____

_____

_____

_____

_____

_____

How will you balance work and play in achieving your dream?

_____

_____

_____

_____

Is there anything you would like to change, right now?

_____

_____

_____

_____

Roadblock: Fear of Failure

Defeat is not the worst of failures.
Not to have tried is the true failure.
— George E. Woodberry, 1855-1930, writer and critic

Results? Why, man, I have gotten lots of results. I know several thousand things that won't work.
If I find 10,000 ways something won't work, I haven't failed. I am not discouraged, because every wrong attempt discarded is another step forward.
— Thomas Edison, 1847-1931, inventor, scientist, and businessman

At this point, it is time to look at another possible obstacle that could tempt you to quit or keep your dream smaller than it could be: the fear of failure. I will show you that it is by looking at your fears that you gain power over them.

What will happen if you fail? People may judge you as being foolish to have even tried. You may judge yourself as being inadequate, or even stupid for trying. Will someone stop loving you, or respecting you? How can you endure another disappointment?

Your greatest fear of failure is:

_____

_____

_____

_____

How have you punished yourself for failure(s) in the past? Do you feel anyone else punished you?

_____

_____

_____

_____

What did you, or could you, learn from your failure(s)?

_____

_____

_____

_____

How could you handle it if you failed again?

_____

_____

_____

_____

Are there any different choices you would like to make?

_____

_____

_____

_____

One of my greatest fears has been, "What will people think?" After many years of struggling with this one, I now know that people will think whatever they want to. Some people will focus on the good and some will see only weakness or negativity. It is their choice of focus and it says more about them than it does about me. It is my choice what I choose to listen to. Generally, I have found critics are people who feel powerless. They try to steal your power by criticizing and making you feel as small as they do. I have found it helpful to quietly send them a blessing of power, which helps free us both.

Back in October of 2004, I raised all my courage and stood in a room of my peers. I publicly announced that I was going to Mexico to write a book. I was taking a month away from my business. I don't know what those people thought, but I do know what I imagined them thinking: "Who does she think she is? What does she know? Her business is going to suffer. What makes her think she can write a book?" I imagined that everyone was sitting around waiting for me to fail, but I reminded myself that I couldn't really fail.

Whatever the outcome, I gave myself a month away from work and away from winter. I had new experiences. I learned new things. I increased my knowledge and my skills. I met some wonderful people. I stretched deeper into myself than I had ever felt possible. I risked exposing myself. I was willing to have a larger and more passionate experience of life. I can now call myself a published author. How could all of that be failure?

You see, the crucial point is that I was not attached to the result. It was the experience I was drawn to. I gave myself permission to fail and therefore, there was no way for me to fail. All I had to do was show up for the journey. No one can ever take away your experiences and that is what an exciting, full, and passionate journey is all about!

Look at how you drive your car. You don't just point it down the road and it drives straight. A car is off course more than 90% of the time. You have to keep adjusting the wheel to keep it on course. And so, too, you have to make adjustments on your life journey.

Another of my fascinating friends in Mexico is an internationally acclaimed artist. In 1994, he was a rich man. In 1995 the peso was devalued and he was a pauper. Realizing that he needed to take action to save his family, he moved everyone to Dallas, Texas, but nothing happened for him there. Not only were his prospects not good, he didn't have any! Again he uprooted his family and moved them to New York. Through the most unusual circumstances, involving a cab driver and 20 painting of Cadillacs for a car show, he was eventually discovered. He now lives back in Mexico, feels secure in his future and considers himself very rich. Had he given up on his dream in Dallas, he would still be there waiting tables for a living.

You have these same choices to make: to let a few setbacks stop you, or to continue towards success. There is something else that can happen as you move towards your goals—you may lose energy for them. You may feel that what once filled you with excitement and drive no longer holds any attraction for you. The magnetism is gone. Some may think that you have to push through this place, but that is very hard to do. Instead of swimming upstream, I prefer to listen to the energy and take my cues there. When the energy disappears I know it is time to take a different approach. Perhaps it is time to rest or take a look at a roadblock that is presenting itself.

After I had spent the first month in Mexico working on my book, I returned to Canada to find that I no longer had any energy for the project. I could not drag myself to sit in front of the computer every Saturday morning after a week's work at the office. Unfortunately, I have seen far too many people give up at this point. A change in energy is a signal that we need to shift—not quit. While I could not continue to write, I kept an eye out for bits of information or insights that showed up in my life. I collected quotations and attended workshops. While some might label this as avoidance, I like to think of it as a gestation period. I was letting go of my agenda and opening to something much better. Had I pushed through and self-published my book, I would not have entered the "Write Stuff" competition. I received so much more, because I followed the energy. I did what felt right for me, and took each step as it presented itself.

Over the next seven days, continue taking steps towards your dream. Continue writing for 15 minutes a day. Even though you have completed the 21-Day Process and the seeds of your dream life have been firmly planted, journalling for 15 minutes a day, every day, is a habit that will continue your growth and evolution. Write about your dreams. Write about how you are enjoying the journey to your dream. Write about the perceived blunders in life and reframe them into stepping stones making you the person you are today. What are you seeing? What are you learning? How are you feeling? Write about whatever is important to you each day. Write about what you want.

Even if your action steps do not immediately achieve your desired goal, you are a success because you have done something new, something that took courage. Stepping through a fear and stretching your abilities builds self-confidence and inner strength. It also improves your life energy and health. Reward yourself! I have found that even a few kind and supportive words to myself are a real reward. We often long to hear words of love and support from others, forgetting that we never give them to ourselves. Becoming my own champion has opened the door for others to champion me as well.

**Affirmation: I choose to be happy!
I choose to celebrate all that I am and all that I do.**

WEEK 9
Choose Your Cheerleader: Support for the Journey

Everyone's got it in him, if he'll only make up his mind and stick at it. None of us is born with a stop-valve on his powers or with a set of limit to his capacities. There is no limit possible to the expansion of each one of us.
— Charles M. Schwab, 1862-1939, industrialist

For those times that you are down and discouraged, you need a cheerleader to help keep you moving. I use the word cheerleader instead of mentor on purpose. A mentor guides or teaches you. It's important that you don't have someone telling you what you should do. This is *your* journey. A cheerleader is a person who is cheering for you, who believes in you and your dreams; someone who will praise and support you, especially when you get discouraged, because with your bigger goals, you will feel discouraged sometimes. In fact, if you never encounter any doubt, you could be shortchanging yourself. Reach for higher goals.

Changing your life involves learning many new lessons. Learning involves course corrections and that is where your cheerleader will come in handy. You will want someone who will tell the truth when you need a course correction. This special someone won't fall for your excuses. They will support you to keep moving even when you are tempted to turn back. For this reason, your cheerleader must also be someone that you trust, respect, and listen to. If you know of someone who fits the bill, and also has achieved what you are going after, all the better.

List three people you know who could possibly fulfill this job for you, on the left hand side.

_____   _____

_____   _____

_____   _____

On the right hand side, write why you would choose them.

In the middle, number them in the order of your preference.

Choose your #1 Cheerleader

How often would you like to meet with your cheerleader? Once a week? Once every two weeks? Once a month? Don't schedule your meetings farther apart than once a month. If the date of a meeting has to be changed, reschedule it as soon as possible. Do not just wait for the next scheduled meeting. Two months is too long to go without support.

Thinking of this person, what do you have to exchange with them for their time and energy? Perhaps you could pay them for their time or buy them lunch. Perhaps you have expertise in an area that they would like some help with. Perhaps this person is also working towards some goals, and you could be cheerleaders for each other. If you want to create something that will generate a profit for you, you could offer a percentage of your profits, when the money arrives. What is this kind of support worth to you? If you do not value their time, they will not really value your goals and dreams.

This week, obtain a committed cheerleader and have your first meeting. If your #1 choice is hesitant, work down the list. If you find that none of the three are excited about the project, you are either not offering enough in exchange, or have chosen the wrong people. Do not to move on to the next chapter until you are working with a cheerleader.

Master Minding

An alternate idea is a Master Mind Group, a powerful tool to help you achieve your goals. Master Minding has been used by many super achievers for decades. Even Napoleon Hill in his famous book, *Think and Grow Rich,* mentions the tremendous benefits of Master Minding. Working with two or more people, each partner supports the other members of the group in their desire. There is no judgment, there is just support. While the structure of your meetings can vary, ensure that the process that I describe is the foundation. I have worked with groups where we talk for two hours and share much about our lives. I have also worked with groups where we only did the basic program and were done within half an hour. I have worked with groups that changed some of the words. Some groups have everyone recite each step. Some have only one person at a time, and some use a combination. I don't believe that there is any right or wrong way as long as you stick to the basic process and share without judgment.

The people you choose to be in your group (minimum three, maximum six) should have the same qualifications as a cheerleader. All members should be working on their own goals and dreams. I suggest a Master Mind Group as a second option because I have found that they can sometimes lose focus. A single cheerleader, focused on you, is usually best. However, a very powerful combination is a cheerleader that you meet with monthly, and a Master Mind Group that meets weekly.

At your first meeting, lay out your destination and plan as

you know it today. Tell your cheerleader or Master Mind Group what steps you are committed to achieving by your next meeting. Write it down so no one forgets. Complete your part of the exchange.

Here is a format that can be helpful when opening these meetings:

1. **I surrender**

   I admit that apart from a higher power, I do not have the power to solve my problems, to improve my life. I need help.

2. **I believe**

   I come to believe that only in my oneness with a higher power, or "Master Mind" can I truly change my life.

3. **I am ready to be changed**

   I realize that erroneous, self-defeating thinking is the cause of my problems, unhappiness, fears, and failures. I am ready to have my beliefs and attitudes changed so my life can be transformed.

4. **I decide to be changed**

   I make a decision to surrender my will and my life to a higher power. I ask to be changed at depth

5. **I forgive**

   I forgive myself for all my mistakes and shortcomings. I also forgive all other persons who appear to have harmed me.

6. **I ask**

   I make known my specific requests while asking my partners' support in knowing that a higher power is fulfilling my needs. (Partners may respond with affirmation such as: "I know that you have been heard and you will experience your demonstration.")

7. **I give thanks**
I give thanks that a higher power is responding to my needs and I feel the joy of my requests being fulfilled right now.

8. **I dedicate my life**
I now have a covenant in which it is agreed that a higher power is supplying me with an abundance of all things necessary to live a successful and happy life.

I dedicate myself to be of maximum service to a higher power and those around me, to live in a manner that sets the highest example for others to follow and to remain responsive to the Universe's guidance.

I go forth with a spirit of enthusiasm, excitement, and expectancy. I am at peace.

Roadblock: Independence

If you have any resistance to this week's assignment, it's because of your independence. Here is an example using stereotypes. Many women just silently hold back a chuckle as they watch their man drive around, frustrated and lost, because he doesn't want to ask for directions. This is characteristic of independence. Independence indicates a resistance to asking for help and a resistance to appear needy. Often your fear of rejection or abandonment may cause you to ask someone other than the person you really want to be your cheerleader. The same thing often happens when people are dating. They end up with someone who doesn't threaten them, but doesn't excite them either: they have lowered their expectations. They may end up settling for someone in their comfort zone instead of a passionate life and partner. This is a huge road-block to receiving wealth in any area of life.

Do you have a problem asking for help/directions/a favour/a date? (Remember to fill in all the lines.)

_____

_____

_____

_____

_____

_____

_____

How could you change your point of view about this?

_____

_____

_____

_____

_____

_____

_____

Roadblock: Dependence

The other extreme is the person who can ask for help, but doesn't feel they have anything to give or offer in exchange. These people are stuck in dependence. They are dependent on others without knowing that they themselves are connected to the source of all good things. Feeling needy, they hoard the good in their lives. In the extreme, they can end up stopping the flow of good into their lives and exacerbate the feeling of not having or being enough.

If you think you are better at asking for help than giving it (ask a friend to confirm this), I suggest that you practice giving. Even if you think you don't have anything to give, just find small ways to brighten someone else's day. Hold an elevator door. Smile, even at strangers. Pick up trash in your neighbourhood. Take soup to a sick friend. Find little ways to give, without expecting anything in return. Give money to your church or charity.

Wherever you are afraid to give freely, you believe that you do not have enough. Is there enough time? Or money? Or energy?

_____

_____

_____

_____

_____

_____

_____

Underlying a belief that you don't have enough is a deeper belief that on your own you are not enough. That is a lie. Joy is found in true giving. I am excited for you as you practice and expand.

The deeper issue under both the role of the Independent and the Dependent is a feeling of being valueless. When we don't value ourselves, we don't see how we could be of value to someone else. We will look deeper at these roadblocks in Week 12.

Strive to balance both giving and asking in your world. Can you do both at least once each day? I know you can! Practice until you complete this week's assignment of finding a cheerleader or Master Mind group and having your first meeting. Have a great week increasing your ability to receive by giving and asking.

In this week's Road Log, focus on any resistance you have to asking or giving. Write for 15 minutes a day and see what you learn.

**Affirmation: I have enough. I do enough.
I am enough!**

WEEK 10
Money Matters

OK. You have chosen your destination and you have committed to taking the trip, but how are you going to pay for it? Do you have enough money? Do you need to accumulate more? Will you earn money along the way? Will you borrow money? One of the greatest causes of failure in business is being underfinanced. The same is true in life. Without enough money, you may be tempted to quit well before you have even travelled halfway to your destination. As a Certified Financial Planner, I know that the secret to success is to have a plan. I want my clients to have rich and rewarding lives now and later. That takes some planning.

Where are You Starting From?

With any journey, you have to know where you are in order to figure out how to get where you want to go. This week will be about looking at where you are starting from financially. I know some of you have been waiting for this part and some of you have been dreading it. I'll show you how to deal with it in a really easy way.

Make a list of your *assets* (what you own) and their current value. Do not include personal items like your TV, clothes, furniture or household effects that will have little or no financial value when you are finished with them. I have included some examples to get you started.

House $_____

Cottage $_____

Vehicle $_____

2nd Vehicle $_____

Retirement savings $_____

Short-term savings $_____

Bank account $_____

Other investments $_____

                       $_____

    Your Total Assets are $_____

Now look at what you owe. These debts are called *lia-bilities.*

Mortgage $_____

Cottage mortgage $_____

Vehicle loan $_____

2nd Vehicle lease $_____

Line of credit $_____

Credit cards $_____

                       $_____

Others $_____

                       $_____

    Your Total Liabilities are $_____

Total Assets - Your Total Liabilities = Your Net Worth

                          $_____

In one year, what do you want your net worth to be?

                          $_____

How will you make that happen?

_____

_____

_____

_____

Add this to your list of goals. Mark your calendar for six months from now. On that date, do this exercise again to determine if you are making progress towards your goal. My advice is to measure your net worth at least once every six months. I have a computer program that tracks my net worth on a daily basis although I only update the bigger assets (like home) values every year.

This is the same process that companies go through to create their balance sheet. See, you are already learning accounting. The other accompanying accounting report is the income statement. It is a record of the earned money brought into a company for a set period of time, and also a record of the money spent.

Your task this week is to produce a Monthly Income Statement and a new budget.

1. How much income did you bring in last month?
$_____ (Net after deductions). If your income fluctuates each month, look at finding an average monthly income over the year.

2. Fixed Monthly Expenses
Make a list of your fixed monthly expenses. Last month's bank statement may be a good place to start looking for these items. List credit card payments only if you are paying off a

carry forward balance i.e. you do not pay off your credit cards each month.

Mortgage/ Rent	$_____
Utilities	$_____
Cottage mortgage	$_____
Property taxes	$_____
Vehicle loan	$_____
Insurance	$_____
2nd vehicle lease	$_____
Line of credit	$_____
Credit card	$_____
	$_____
Other _____	$_____

Total fixed monthly expenses are $_____

3. Your Income - Total Fixed Payments
    = Your Discretionary Income $_____

Talk to your Financial Planner (covered in Week 16) about how to increase your discretionary income, and if it would be in your best interest to do so.

4. On a yearly basis, how much do you spend on:
(Do not include items if you pay them monthly. They will be recorded later.)

Car maintenance	$_____
Personal insurance	$_____
Car insurance	$_____
Savings	$_____
Home maintenance	$_____

Home insurance $_____

Vacations $_____

Gifts $_____

Other $_____

    Total yearly expenses are $_____

Take your total yearly expenses divided by 12 and place that number in the calculation below. See the asterisk*

    Total yearly expense/ 12 = $_____*

5. Discretionary Expenses

Now, let's look at where you are spending your discretionary income. Your last month's bank statement and credit card statement are still good sources of this information.

Groceries $_____

Short-term savings $_____

Clothing $_____

Mid-term savings $_____

Hair cuts $_____

Retirement savings $_____

Other savings $_____

Restaurant meals $_____

Pet expenses $_____

School expenses $_____

Child care $_____

Home maintenance $_____

Other $_____

1/12 Yearly Expenses*

(from exercise 4) $_____

Your Total Discretionary Expenses $_____

6. Calculate

Discretionary Income (#3) - Discretionary Expenses (#5)

= _____

If you have a positive number (more income than expenses) then you are "leaking cash," you are spending money without knowing where it's going. If you have a negative amount, you are spending more than you are making.

Many people are shocked at how much money they spend on unknowns. If you would like to find out where it is all going, carry a small notepad with you for the next week. In this notebook, jot down every cent you spend. I know the information will surprise you. Calculate how much money you are spending each year on various "unknowns" such as coffees, magazines, newspapers, parking, music, etc. If you feel that you do not have any money to contribute to your longer term goals, this exercise is a must. You will feel differently when you are done. Then make some choices. For example, is your weekly magazine more important than financing your dream?

What do you think about your current Balance Sheet and Income Statement?

_____

_____

_____

_____

Are there any changes that you would like to make?

_____

_____

Where are you going?

What do you want your net worth to be in five years?

_____

What do you need your net worth to be in ten years?

_____

At what age do you want to be financially independent
(when you no longer have to work to maintain your desired
income)? _____

How much money will you need to be financially independent? _____

How will you get there?

How will you achieve that amount?

_____

_____

_____

_____

_____

_____

How much money are you willing to commit to your
goals each month?

_____

_____

_____

Where will it come from?

_____

_____

_____

_____

The Advisor's Edge, May 2005 reported on the 2005 Sco-tiabank/IPSOS-Reid Study:

- 61% of Canadians agree they began saving for retirement much too late and wish they had started earlier.
- 55% say they would have saved more, but they were living from paycheque to paycheque. (I know people who make $250,000 a year who tell me this!)

Affirmation: I choose to be happy! I always have more money than I need.

WEEK 11

All good things want to be given to you today, if you have the willingness to receive them. Your receiving will allow you to give at a much higher level, which in turn, will allow you more receiving at an even higher level. So everything will move forward for you and everyone.
— Chuck Spezzano, author and workshop facilitator

Roadblock: Fear of Money

Many people scoff when I ask them why they are afraid of having more money. I'm devoting an entire chapter to this subject because, although most people say they want more money, they are only comfortable with the amount of money they usually have. In the sales business it is widely known that if you take a high performing salesperson and put them in a poor producing region, in a relatively short period of time they will increase business so that they return to their previous income. The opposite also works. If you put a poor producing sales person in a highly productive region, over time the sales will fall off until they are back within their earning comfort zone. Wherever you are, you are in your money comfort zone. The reasoning about how much money you have is buried deep within your subconscious. If you do not believe me, just take a look.

The trouble with money is:

_____

_____

The trouble with money is:

_____

_____

The trouble with money is:

_____

_____

The trouble with money is:

_____

_____

The trouble with money is:

_____

_____

Think about a few people who have a lot of money and power. Perhaps they are in your circle of acquaintances, perhaps in your community. Also think of very rich people in the news—Donald Trump, the Kennedys, the Royal family.

List ten rich and powerful people.

_____

_____

_____

_____

_____

_____

_____

_____

_____

_____

What do you think about people who have money? People who have power?

_____

_____

_____

_____

_____

_____

What do you think about people who own big businesses?

_____

_____

_____

_____

_____

How do you think they got that much money? Power?

_____

_____

_____

_____

_____

_____

_____

_____

What did your parents think about people with money?
With power?

_____

_____

_____

_____

_____

_____

_____

How did your parents sacrifice themselves for money?
For power? What did they give up? What did you lose because of their choices around money and power?

_____

_____

_____

_____

Do you respect people with money? Yes or No

Do you respect people with power? Yes or No

I know a woman who has a hard time trusting people, especially those with businesses. She believes that they are out to take advantage of poor, unsuspecting customers. She has a form of scarcity consciousness. She would never let herself have a business. Her only choice was to limit herself to a paycheque. Yes, business people are in business to make money, but then again, don't employees also work for money? Being an employee, in and of itself, does not make you a person of integrity. Being a business person does not make you dishonest. You are who you are, no matter how much money you have, or don't have. Integrity is not related to money.

I know that logically what I have said makes perfect sense, but it is important for you to uncover the judgments you hold against people with money or power. If you judge others for their money or power, you will never allow yourself to possess either. If you have a history of grievances against those in authority (teachers, bosses, politicians, etc.), this is an especially important area for you to look at. Rebels never make great leaders because great leaders also know when and how to be great followers.

Many people have a lot of power and money issues tied together. The reason for this is that they let people with money have power over them. In some way, they have sold themselves out. They have given up their power to someone, or some business, that was (as they believed at the time) the source of their money and therefore, the source of whatever value they attribute to money (like security, fun, survival, respect).

For example, have you ever worked at a job you didn't like? How did it make you feel?

_____

_____

_____

_____

_____

_____

What have you done for money that went against your personal values?

_____

_____

_____

_____

_____

_____

_____

Why did you do it? What was your justification?

_____

_____

_____

_____

_____

How did you feel at the time?

_____

_____

_____

_____

_____

_____

_____

_____

The person who instructed you to go against your values did not have the power. It was not the money that was the issue. Money did not have the power. You had the power to make a choice. Perhaps it is not the choice you would make today, but you had a choice and you made the best one that you could have made at the time. Forgive and let go. You will make a better choice today.

To those who forgive, all is forgiven.
— Christopher Moon, author and workshop facilitator

Forgive and Let Go

Here is a visualization exercise for forgiveness and letting go. Find a quiet space where you will not be disturbed. Close your eyes. Relax and breathe deeply for a minimum of ten breaths before beginning the visualization. Relax some more. Gentle, instrumental music in the background may help you relax. If you record the meditation in your own voice it will deepen your experience. Go slowly and let yourself get truly involved with each scene.

Imagine the person you believe has harmed you standing in front of you. See a black line that connects you to that person. In your mind's eye, have a conversation with them. Ask them how they felt about the situation. Ask them how it affected their life. Ask them how they are today and if it still affects them. Tell them of how it hurt you. Tell them how it affected your life and how it continues to affect you today. Tell them any ways you have secretly been punishing them. Tell them what you wish had happened. Tell them what you have learned. Offer your forgiveness. Tell them that you both have to move past this in your lives. Tell them what you need to move on. See them giving it to you. Tell them that you are sorry for punishing them for so long with your anger. Cut the black line that keeps you attached. Offer your forgiveness. Imagine the two of you sharing a hug or handshake. Then say goodbye and truly wish them well.

Now, imagine yourself locked in a cage, locked in irons. See how helpless you look, how much pain you are in. Now, with the kindness and heart of an angel, see the person you are now going over to that cage, opening the door, and unlocking the chains. Show compassion. Speak loving words to your tortured self. Forgive yourself for holding on to so much anger and for any revenge you may have taken. You have punished yourself enough. Let yourself out of jail and allow your poor battered soul to be bathed in white light. Bring that vision into your heart. When you can feel tenderness, you have done the exercise.

You may want to repeat this exercise whenever you notice that you are feeling angry about something. You will feel freer and lighter when it is done. You will be free to move on in your life.

How will you handle the same situation in the future?

_____

_____

_____

_____

If you judge people harshly just because they have money, or don't have money, you are dealing with "economic prejudice." It is just as ugly as racial or religious prejudice. You are looking at these people through the rear-view mirror of your past experiences and beliefs. Take the time to root out your economic prejudice and free yourself from the limitations it produces.

You're not much help to the poor by being one of them. I like to believe that we are agents of Good and were born to create Heaven on Earth. Each of us has tried in our own way. If we encounter failure, many of us quit to spend the rest of our lives in quiet desperation, trying only to stay safe. I say live! Be that agent for Heaven on Earth. Spiritual activist and author Marianne Williamson has said that it is our light not our darkness that scares us. Jesus told us that we are powerful beyond measure. Where are you powerfully creating Heaven on Earth? What is it that burns in your soul to change? If you had one thing that you would like to teach the world, what would it be?

_____

_____

_____

_____

_____

_____

_____

_____

_____

_____

_____

During your 15 minutes of visualization and writing each morning this week, see yourself in your mind's eye. Send blessings to yourself and see yourself getting taller and taller, bigger and bigger. Let yourself know that it is safe to live a large life. It is safe to be powerful. It is safe to be seen. Now, see yourself on stage, in front of thousands of people, and continue to let yourself grow. Be willing to feel your feelings. Be open to receive love and support from all those people. See yourself living your wildest dream! **See yourself creating Heaven on Earth and then write about it.**

Watch for any places that you may be playing small for your life. Reward yourself with a day just for you. Do something that you have never done before. Make it something you have always been meaning to try. I hope it is something that feels exciting to you. Perhaps a pottery class, maybe a massage. I parachuted out of a plane once. What ever it is, go for it!

**Affirmation: I choose to be happy! I love money and the choices it brings me.
I am willing to be power full.**

WEEK 12

Unless we are living a joyful, loving, and creative adventure, we are living a life dictated by the past and its needs. Vision is a state in which the positive future dictates the present moment. Vision shows the way toward success and brings success energy into the present.
— Chuck Spezzano, author and workshop facilitator

Toll Booths: Prices you Pay

When people begin this program, they sometimes have a hard time envisioning big goals. This is because they are playing small in their lives. When you play small, you receive small amounts. Playing small comes from judging yourself as inadequate. I know because I am a recovering perfectionist. Perfectionists have approval and love confused. In the past I felt that I had to be perfect to be of any value and to be loved. Logically this makes no sense, but emotions have little to do with logic. The need to be perfect keeps you small. Afraid to make a mistake, it keeps you from trying anything new. It keeps you stuck, and it certainly blocks you from living the life of your dreams.

The beginning of pain and frustration lies in judgment. Whenever you enter into judgmental thinking, you create experiences of inadequacy, guilt, and shame. It does not matter if you judge yourself or others. Any feelings of guilt and shame create a feeling of being valueless. Whenever we hold on to guilt and shame, we invite punishment into our lives.

We also condemn ourselves to repeating the same old patterns.

As a young child, I was sexually abused for many years by a friend of the family. I grew up with intense feelings of guilt and shame. What I took from that experience was the belief that my only value to men was in being sexual. As a young adult, I kept delivering what I believed men valued, hoping that they would love me in return. Just like a gambling addiction, I hit the jackpot often enough that it continued to reinforce my belief. After a date rape, I finally saw that something was terribly wrong and I knew it was me. The good news was that this was the start of my spiritual journey. Combining love, understanding, and forgiveness is the only way out of guilt and shame. It was only through forgiving myself and the men in my life that I could become healthier. Once I chose love and understanding, I could then move to forgiveness.

When you judge yourself, you create guilt, which leaves you feeling critical of yourself and others. These judgments come from rules that you have learned and followed throughout your life, the programming of what you have been told you should do. You measure yourself and your performance against these rules and this programming. Many of these rules were instilled in you when you were very young—not the best time to make lifelong decisions for yourself. These rules build your comfort zone, the familiar experience of life that you feel safe and secure in. It is a trap. It has a level that we will not let ourselves sink below and also a level that we do not let ourselves rise above. Left unchallenged, we condemn ourselves to a life of mediocrity.

In my family, I learned the best way to stay out of trouble was to try to be as invisible as possible. At that time, children were to been seen and not heard. I did everything to follow the family rules. Some of those rules have been instrumental in my creating a good life for myself. Some rules have held me back. Some rules were conflicting. We were taught to always do our best. Unfortunately, my child mind heard that as: "Be perfect." I worked harder and harder. At the age of 14, I became one of four junior members of the Manitoba 4H Club Council. Through it, I got to travel to various cities for meetings and developed a love of travel that continues today. My parents were very proud of me.

But then I broke an unspoken family rule by winning a beauty pageant. That rule was do well, but not so well that your sister feels bad about herself. My father was sure it was going to ruin me. Girlfriends shunned me. I felt negatively judged everywhere. Maybe I was too full of myself, I don't know, but the message I got was: "Don't shine too much." Well, how much is too much? Not knowing that answer, I retreated, pulled back, and tried to stay small. I intentionally sabotaged my participation in the next round of competition in the Miss Manitoba Pageant. I didn't want to win because of what it had cost me to win the previous pageant.

To this day, when I start to receive a lot of attention or "win too much," I start to feel nervous, and I subconsciously wait for the judgment or punishment. I get outside of my comfort zone and my programming tells me that the situation is dangerous. The fear tries to control me. I am tempted to stop growing and stay small and safe.

By trying to avoid the threat of pain, you close down. Your life shrinks and so do you. The real juice of life comes from stretching past the feeling of comfortable into exciting. This is where life is really lived—outside of your comfort zone! The purpose of this program is to assist you to choose new experiences and get uncomfortable. Even taking a little step will bring back your passion. Living large can feel very risky, and very exhilarating. It is a leap towards leadership. We need more leaders. What a wonderful example for your children.

You can never be perfect because as you learn any skill, you always see the next step. You start to see how you could have done it better. The fact is, you are always doing the very best that you can do at any given moment.

It took me a long time to learn how to ski. I didn't start until I was about 27 and I had never been very coordinated when it came to sports. My initial experience on the ski hill was a day spent falling down and picking myself up. Had I judged my efforts as less than perfect, I would have quit. But instead, I chose to congratulate myself for each improvement. I kept going. Eventually I became a pretty good intermediate skier. For nearly ten years, skiing became my passion. I travelled to an exotic ski destination every year: Banff, Whistler, Vail, Austria, Switzerland, and Italy became my playgrounds. I would have missed out on so much if I had demanded that I be a perfect skier the first day out. So it is for any journey: you need patience, dedication, and practice. As you focus on the experience and let go of your attachment to results, you can enjoy the journey and keep going.

Where have you been less than perfect in your life? Which of your life rules were/are you breaking? What do you still feel guilty about?

_____

_____

_____

_____

_____

_____

What were/are you trying to achieve with this behavior? Did you get it?

_____

_____

_____

_____

How would you have preferred to handle it differently? How could you have been more successful in achieving your desire?

_____

_____

_____

_____

_____

_____

_____

What lesson did you learn from making this/these mistakes?

_____

_____

_____

_____

_____

_____

How can you incorporate this lesson into your life now? Who do you want to be?

_____

_____

_____

_____

Is there any action you need to do to undo any harm?

_____

_____

_____

_____

Debt

Are you willing to go into debt to achieve any of your dreams? _____

What are the reasons, justifications, and considerations around your answer?

_____

_____

_____

_____

_____

_____

There is no right or wrong answer here. Each answer can be valid for a variety of reasons. Later, I will discuss the idea of working with a financial planner and he or she will be able to evaluate how advantageous the use of debt is in your situation. Sometimes debt can be used to your advantage, such as when you use it to acquire or build an appreciating asset. Acquiring debt for depreciating assets or expenses isn't usually advised. If you were to ask me "Should I go into debt, or use my retirement savings?" I would probably suggest using debt. Remember, it is not always just about the numbers. I would suggest acquiring debt instead of using your retirement savings because you are more likely to pay someone else back than yourself. You also have to include the emotional side of the situation, without letting emotions dominate. Balance both the logical and emotional side of each question or direction.

There are four ways to make money:
Work for it.
Have others work for it, for you.
Have your money work for you.
Have other people's money work for you.

Once a debt is already in place, I am often asked, "Should I pay off my debts, or should I save?" The answer is always unique to a person's financial and tax situation, but I try to encourage a balance of both and here is why. If you scrimp and save to pay off your debts, how do you feel? Like you put out a lot of cash, but got nothing in return? This is sacrifice. Whenever you allow yourself to sacrifice, you simultaneously build the foundation for indulgence. That is why credit card debt is so hard to get out from under. You pay off the debt, but then feel you need a reward. The credit card continues to be a source of pain and pleasure. Early in my career, I met a couple who had just paid off their mortgage. They were delighted. Instead of starting an investment program, they went on a spending spree. They bought two new cars and a vacation property. Four years later, they are still only saving $50 per month. I have seen this happen time and time again.

When you balance paying off your debt with some investing, you start to expand your comfort zone. You reduce the amount of debt you are comfortable with and you build the experience of having more money saved. As you get comfortable with saving money, you will see how it grows and you will be better able to nurture it. I have found that in all areas of life, balance is the answer.

Debt can be about another price you think you have to pay for something in your past. In other words, we will often acquire financial debt as a result of an emotional debt—either owing to or from us. In workshops, I often ask participants who are struggling with debt, "If this debt was attached to a person, who would it be?" As they trust their intuition, a name will pop into their mind.

If debt has been an issue for you (it is an issue for you if you or your spouse are not happy with it), let's look a little deeper into your unconscious. I believe everything is a gift. You may not like the wrapping, but there is always something in it for you.

Who has hurt you the most? What do you think they owe you for that?

_____

_____

_____

_____

Who do you think you owe, for something you did in the past?

_____

_____

_____

_____

_____

_____

_____

How and who has it hurt to carry these debts with you? If you don't think it has, ask someone close to you.

_____

_____

_____

_____

_____

_____

_____

What are you willing to do about this problem? Let it go, meet with those it's hurt, give to others in your future, etc.

_____

_____

_____

_____

_____

_____

_____

You may want to repeat the **Forgiveness and Letting Go Visualization** (see the Tool Box). Use this exercise whenever you notice that you are feeling guilty about anything. You will feel freer and lighter when it is done. In fact, you will be free to move on in your life. The best part is that when you reduce the debt in your inner world, it will help reduce the debt you carry in your outer world.

This week in your daily writing look at your thoughts, beliefs, and feelings about debt—both financial and emotional debt. Talk to your spouse and friends about it.

**Affirmation: I choose to be happy!
I travel lightly because I forgive and am forgiven.**

WEEK 13
Roadblock: Self-Worth

You get paid what you believe you are worth. You receive what you believe you deserve. I *hated* this truth when I heard it. I fought against it and did not want to believe it. But, in the end, I did. Money is just an exchange. You exchange your labour for what you believe it is worth. If you truly believed that you were worth more, you would be out finding a job, career, or business opportunity that paid you more. Perhaps you believe that you are willing to settle for less money because of all the other benefits of the job. This is wonderful reasoning, as long as you are happy with your income. If you are unsatisfied in any way, it is of the utmost importance that you pay attention to this feeling.

If you want more money, you have to do something to get it. This might be as simple as doing the same thing in a different location or in a different organization. Or it may involve getting more education. It could be a matter of finding a new career. Or it might involve taking on a part-time job or at-home business. Or it might mean building a multinational business. Everything involves taking a risk.

Living life fully is like investing. You want to receive the highest rate of return for the lowest acceptable risk. Having a job with a set income is comparable to a Guaranteed Investment Certificate (GIC). You always know how much you are going to be paid even if it isn't very much. Working on commission or owning your own business is more like investing in the stock market. Yes, you can make much more money, but the amount fluctuates. There is no guaranteed income. It is up to you to find the right balance of both security and opportunity for you and your family.

As with your income level, everything you receive and have is a reflection of what you believe you are worth: Your home, your spouse, the way others treat you, and especially how you treat yourself. Whatever we feel we deserve, we will attract.

Really stretch yourself and your goals and then watch. As you start to play a bigger role in your life, your ability to receive will increase.

In your life, where are you receiving less than you would like?

_____

_____

_____

_____

What would happen if you decided not to settle for this?

_____

_____

_____

_____

What rules would you be breaking by not settling? Who made those rules?

_____

_____

_____

What would you rather have in your life?

_____

_____

_____

_____

_____

_____

_____

_____

What are you willing to do or risk to have it?

_____

_____

_____

_____

Do you believe you can have it? Why or why not?

_____

_____

_____

_____

Fill Your Tank: Giving and Receiving

Now that you've lessened the burden of guilt and debt last week, let's look at how you give and receive—to and from yourself and others.

Early in my practice, I met Bill and Mabel. They were a lovely couple—sweet in every way. They regularly gave 10%

of all they earned to their church. Their children had everything they could give them. Bill and Mabel's children were already starting university. At 45 and 48 respectively, this couple had managed to save only $5,000 throughout their lives. They came to me for help.

The first thing I saw was that they were giving 10% to their church and the rest to their children. There was little left for themselves. They faithfully gave away more than $500 per month to their church, but only saved $50 for themselves. And that was not only true about their money—it was also true about how they lived their lives. What you do with your money reflects what you do with everything. Bill and Mabel gave little of their money, their time, or energy to themselves.

I suggested they start with a better balance (there is that word again). I suggested that they combine what they thought they could manage ($500 and $50) and give half to the church and half to themselves. They would not do it: 10% absolutely had to go to the church. I did not judge their choice. I then looked at the details of their budget to see what else was not essential. They would not let go of anything. They had their reasons and their explanations. As they were unwilling to change anything, I asked them what they wanted from me. They replied that they wanted me to assure them that they could comfortably retire. I could not. They left upset because I could not help them, but, in fact, they were not willing to help themselves. They had so many rules about life; they could not see another way. This is an example of why I ask you to spend so much time uncovering programming in your subconscious mind. You cannot change what you cannot or will not see. As the famous definition of insanity goes, insanity is doing the same things you've always done and expecting different results.

Trapped in their fear of their financial future, Bill and

Mabel were giving from an empty place. Unwilling to alter their situation, they continued to sacrifice their future security for the benefit of others. There was no balance in how much they gave to themselves and how much they gave to others. Were they following rules? What was driving their actions? Why did they value others more than themselves? I can't be sure. But I do know that you can look at behaviours in your life and become aware of your programming so that you can make changes and perhaps better choices.

Where do you put others before you in your life?

_____

_____

_____

_____

What are you going without because of this action?

_____

_____

_____

_____

_____

_____

_____

What is your payoff? What are you trying to gain? (love, approval, acceptance, esteem, power, control, etc)

_____

_____

_____

_____

_____

_____

_____

_____

Perhaps, like Bill and Mabel, you give too much. Giving too much is when you are giving more to others than you give to yourself. This is called sacrifice. Whenever and wherever we are in sacrifice, we begin to feel resentment and then unconsciously want revenge or a payback. When I started to give 10% of my income to my church, I did it because the minister told me that I would be repaid ten times what I had given. It sounded like a good investment to me. I was giving money, so I expected that I would get money back in return. It didn't happen, and I became resentful. I was giving to take. I had an agenda and a demand attached to my giving. I gave from an empty place and that never works. I now give to my church in gratitude for all the gifts I have been given, not in order to try to get more. I give from the fullness of my life. I also give in a lot of other places, all to people and organizations that either feed my soul or display values that I admire.

When you give with an expectation of return, this is giving to take—also called manipulation. When you give because you *should*, you become resentful and start looking for a payback. When you give because you feel full of gratitude for the gifts in your life, with no expectation of return, this is true giving. You can only truly give from a full place.

But what if you are feeling empty? How do you give from this place? Whenever you feel empty, you must prioritize filling up your tank first. What do you need—love, money, food, energy, acceptance, rest? Give it to yourself immediately. It is a common belief that if you feel empty, you should give more. I have found that doing so only leaves me feeling emptier. What do the airlines tell you to do if the oxygen masks fall from the ceiling? Put the mask on yourself first, and then help others.

Notice that I said, "feeling empty." Whether this is grounded in reality doesn't matter, because it is our perception of reality that counts. Giving from an empty feeling will only leave you feeling emptier, and looking for the payback is expecting other people to fill your needs. This leaves you dependent on others to fill you up. As you start feeding yourself, you become less needy. You are your own source of good. As you treat yourself, so the world treats you. As you feed yourself, you feel better and your vibration increases so that you attract better experiences into your life. From this very full place, you can now give back to the world without looking for any reciprocity—you have already received it.

Let's look at your financial affairs. What percentage of your net income do you give to yourself? (Giving to yourself financially means saving for your retirement, not next year's holiday.) Why that amount?

_____

_____

_____

_____

What percentage do you save for you mid-term goals (e.g. new car, home renos)? Why that amount?

_____

_____

_____

_____

Adding up all that you give (donations, gifts, etc.) what percentage of your net income is this? What is your reason for this giving?

_____

_____

_____

_____

Are you feeling financially empty or full? Why?

_____

_____

_____

_____

What percentage of your spare time and energy (not sleeping or working) do you spend on meeting your own needs and desires and doing what you want to do? Why?

_____

_____

_____

_____

What percentage of your spare time and energy do you spend caring for or helping others? Why?

_____

_____

_____

_____

Are you using your time to feed yourself? Others? Are you balanced?

_____

_____

_____

_____

How do you want to redesign your finances so that you are giving to yourself and others in a balanced way?

_____

_____

_____

_____

_____

_____

_____

How do you want to redesign your time and energy so that you are giving to yourself and others in perfect balance?

_____

_____

_____

_____

_____

_____

_____

Looking at your life, where do you feel undernourished? What are you hungry for? What do you need?

_____

_____

_____

_____

_____

_____

_____

What else can you do to feed yourself and keep yourself full?

_____

_____

_____

Talk with your life partner about this section. If you do not have a partner, discuss this with a close friend or family member. In my experience, each of you will feel that you are giving more than you are receiving in one or more areas of your relationship. When you are not mindful, your loving relationship can easily turn into a competition for need gratification. Each of you has needs. Talk about them. Take responsibility for them. Commit to feeding yourself, but also let your partner know how they can help nourish you. Let them experience the gift of giving. Our needs often go unmet because we have danced around the subject. Clear and specific requests work the best. If you ask, without a demand, you just might get it—especially if you are giving to yourself as well. Find out what your spouse truly wants from you. Come up with a plan to help make your relationship more satisfying for both of you.

I have often heard it said that the success of a relationship is in direct proportion to the ability of the relationship to meet both parties' needs. Listen to your inner guidance and only say yes to what feels true for you. Ask the same of your partner. It will probably take some time to find peace on a few subjects, but stick with it. As always, start with easy steps first. I know that it will bring you much closer together. Or, the possibility of having a successful relationship will become abundantly clear. Either way, you will be able to have greater clarity about getting what you really want from one of the most important relationships in your life. You deserve it!

This week, begin each day with the Giving and Receiving Meditation below. Ask for what you want, and give of yourself, at least once a day. Make your asking and giving a stretch. A stretch is doing something that you would not normally do. It is taking the next step. Record your findings in your Road Log.

Giving And Receiving Meditation

Here is a meditation that I use to increase my ability to receive. When I start with using my mind to expand my ability to receive, matching results start to show up in my life. Just through using my mind to receive, I magically have fewer needs and wants. I feel more fulfilled. As I receive, I naturally have more to truly give. As I truly give, I open to receive even more.

Go to a quiet place where you will not be interrupted. Play soft instrumental music if that helps you relax. Close your eyes. Relax. Take a minimum of ten long, deep breaths. Relax even more with every exhalation. Imagine a white line of energy coming through the top of your head, joining you with Heaven. Imagine another white line of energy flowing up through your feet, anchoring you to the Earth. See both energy strands filling you with love and peace. You are receiving from Heaven and from Earth, and you are filled.

See your heart opening and the white energy flowing out into the world. One at a time, let the people in your life appear in your mind's eye. Look deep into their eyes and send your white light from your heart to theirs. This white light is your wish to send them love. You may also wish to send them various other blessings as well. Please feel free to do so. Then see that they are also sending you their white blessings of love. Be open to intuit if they are also sending you other blessings. Thank them and allow the next person to appear.

See your mother, your father, each of your siblings, your partner, your children, your friends, and anyone else who appears in your mind's eye. When you feel complete with this portion, allow yourself to see them all as a group. See your white energy of love surrounding them and protecting them.

Now, feel them sending you their white energy of love to surround and protect you.

As you go through the day, you can do a short form of this visualization. With practice, you will be able to be connected to Heaven in a heartbeat. Just open your heart, send the white line of energy, and share a blessing with someone. It will come back to you in ways you could never have imagined! You can also use this meditation to open your heart and receive whatever dream or goal you desire.

Affirmation: I choose to be happy! I receive abundantly and I give generously.

WEEK 14
Roadblock: Fear of Loss

Helen Keller, the blind/deaf author and lecturer said:

Security is mostly a superstition. It does not exist in nature, nor do the children of men as a whole experience it. Avoiding danger is no safer in the long run than outright exposure. Life is either a daring adventure, or nothing.

Fear of loss can hold you back in two ways. In one, you fear that you have to give up something that you value in order to take your next step. In the other, you fear that if you actually achieved your heart's desire, you would not survive the pain of losing it. Both are roadblocks to your success.

Whatever your desire, what do you think you might lose by achieving it? How about time with your family? Will you lose friends if you become more affluent? Will you have to lose your current income? Will you have to leave a relationship? Really flesh this out.

_____

_____

_____

_____

A dilemma is when you cannot choose between options. Perhaps you dream of becoming an artist but are afraid to become a "starving artist." You want to be creative and be financially secure, too. All the choices you can see to make feel like losses. Do not despair. If you feel that you must lose something, then you have not yet dug deep enough. There is another choice. There are options that you have not yet seen. Ask yourself questions, like "How can I be an artist and still be financially secure?" Write down each and every answer, no matter how crazy it appears. With diligence you will find the answer. If the answer has any feeling of loss attached, you do not have the right answer yet.

How can I _____ and still
_____?

A great way to work through this conflict is to use the Integration Exercise from the Tool Box. Another exercise is to see each side of the conflict or dilemma as a "mini-you." Hold a side in each of your hands, and then let them talk to each other. As an example, let's say part of me loves to be out in public, socializing till the wee hours of the morning and another side of me likes to be home alone, watching TV, and cuddled up in bed before ten. When a friend asks me to go to a party, both sides of me can be fighting for control. I use this exercise to hear both sides. I let one part of me express its needs while the other part listens. They often find an answer that works for both of them, as I move my hands together as in the above exercise. Whenever you are having difficulty making a decision, try this exercise. It will help you to move forward.

What if you want to live in California and your partner wants to live in New York? Keep looking for a way for both of you to win. Winning is when you both get what you want. If only one partner wins, then the other must lose. When we chose to be the loser, we will get revenge in another way. Do not settle for what you don't want. Don't let yourself be a loser in any way. Don't let your partner be a loser in any way. Persist until you have found an answer that feels like a win for both of you.

If possessions, positions, or people are right and true for you, you will not lose them. They will travel right alongside you. If they choose not to travel with you, then they are holding you back. Is that what you really want? Do not use relationships as an excuse to hold back. The unconscious revenge you take on them will destroy what you have anyway. Take the example of keeping a job just for the money. Far too many times, I hear people make that excuse for not moving forward in their lives: they cannot afford to lose the income. If your job (or relationship, or home decor, or anything) does not feed your spirit, it is depleting you. It will make you smaller. You will end up unhappy and embittered. It will be a downward spiral and the money that has resulted from the sale of your spirit will never be worth it.

Now I am not suggesting that you up and do anything drastic like quit your job without a plan, but once you have a plan and it is working, do not stay a moment longer in a career that does not satisfy you. Ensure you discuss this with your financial planner.

How are you playing win/lose in your life?

_____

_____

_____

_____

What can or will you do to create win/win situation(s) in this/these area(s)?

_____

_____

_____

_____

_____

_____

_____

Now, what happens if you achieve your goal and then lose it? The truth is that you can never lose what you truly value. Far too often, I listen to people who lament and cry about a lost relationship. As I was writing this book, I was staying with a woman who was distraught because her boyfriend dumped her. She was so upset that she did not know how she could go on. Two years before, I had met them as a couple. Each time one of them left the room, the other complained about how awful the absent one was. Is this any way to treat someone that you value? If you truly desire and love someone, you need to treat them with love and respect.

Eventually, we lose our partners through death. How will you ever survive that loss? If you are afraid of a broken heart, you already have one. We have all felt the pain of losing a loved one. Instead of focusing on the loss, one could choose to focus on the gain. You had the privilege of spending many years with that special person. You received their gifts and shared much joy. As you do focus on your gratitude for this person, your heart will lighten. This is another example of how pain is a given, but suffering is optional.

Is there anyone that you are still hanging onto? Consider your first love. If you have not experienced a deeper love than that, you are still hanging on to them in your mind.

_____

_____

_____

_____

To help release this attachment, do the **Forgiveness and Letting Go Meditation** in the Tool Box. Once you have let go, truly open your heart to your next love.

Looking at your dream, who must you become to achieve it?

_____

_____

_____

_____

What must you release to do so?

_____

_____

_____

_____

F-E-A-R is False Evidence Appearing Real

What is your greatest fear around money?

_____

_____

_____

_____

_____

_____

_____

Between one and one hundred, what are the chances this could really come true? Why?

_____

_____

_____

_____

In my workshops, participants usually tell me that their greatest fear is becoming a bag lady or a homeless person. What are the real chances of that happening to you? If you are following this program, I know it won't. But the fact remains that there are people running around who are driven by various unrealistic fears. Some fears aren't even yours. You inherited them! This widespread fear of homelessness (especially in North America) is left over from our family members who survived the Great Depression. Could that happen again? I can't say, but I do know that worrying about it isn't going to stop it. Left unaddressed and out of balance, this fear can create a prison for you because there is never enough money to calm this fear.

Worrying about a fear actually helps create it. This fear will drive you to cling to money as your source of security, but when you are connected to a source or spirit or God or Creator, you have access to everything! Clinging to money will make you act in ways that will actually cost you. You will make costly investment decisions, limit your experience of life, and limit your happiness. Attachment to money may keep your money under the mattress and force you to pass up lucrative business opportunities. You may miss the joy of a fun holiday with your family. You may lose relationships with real people because you are so attached to your wallet. If you have ever feared losing a relationship, you know how any clinging just pushes people away. It works the same way in every area of life, including money. So let's discover a few of those unconscious beliefs.

I am not saying that becoming a street person could not happen to you. You could also be killed in a car accident, but does that stop you from driving? There is the occasional plane crash, but does that stop you from flying? My aunt doesn't fly and I certainly see how that limits her visits with her family and her experience of seeing the rest of the world. In most cases, the chances of becoming a street person are very small. Yes, having limited funds does limit your choices, but that is why I have written this book. I want you to have enough money to live out all your dreams.

Here is a quick way to begin looking at any fear.

What is the reality of this fear happening?

_____

_____

_____

_____

If it did happen, how would you handle it? What would you do?

_____

_____

_____

_____

_____

_____

_____

_____

Although you might not like it, could you survive it?

_____

_____

_____

_____

Back in May 1981, I had a great job in the oil industry. I had just bought my first home the year before. Mortgage rates were 18% and I had two roommates living with me to support the payments. I was enjoying a new boyfriend. By the end of June, I had been laid off my job, my roommates had both moved out, and my boyfriend had died in a motor vehicle accident. I only had $8,000, and the mortgage payments were more than $2,000 a month. I was devastated, to say the least, but I realized that as long as I lived in Canada, I would always have a roof over my head and food to eat. Yes, I would prefer something better, but in the worst case scenario, I would survive. At that moment, I realized I was safe and I went beyond survival mode. The fear lifted and I could clearly see the choices I had to make. Fear blinds you and cripples you. It keeps you stuck. It is said that at the end of our lives, it is not the things we did that we most regret, we regret the things we didn't do.

Since 1981, my abundance has continued to build. I am no longer running away from my fear. I addressed it and it no longer has any power over me. I now make my conscious choices based on what I want to create, not want I want to avoid.

Let's look at one of your truly big ideas—one that scares the pants off you. What is it? (Again, if you don't have one, you are not stretching enough.)

_____

_____

_____

_____

If you really went for it, and it didn't work, what is the worst thing that could happen?

_____

_____

_____

_____

Could you survive it?

_____

Could you rebuild from it?

_____

Over the next seven days, examine your fears. Ask again and again: "What am I afraid of?" If nothing comes to you, ask "If I were to pretend that I was afraid of something, what would it be?" Once you have a subject, ask yourself various related questions like "Why?"and "Where did that come from?" Learn as much as you can about it.

Perhaps you have been procrastinating, and fear has been stopping you from taking the next step. Decide if that fear is still relevant in your life. Do you want to keep it, or let it go? If dumping it is not easy, there is still more for you to learn from it. Once you have learned what you need to learn and are comfortable with the process, releasing your fear happens naturally.

This week, take a step toward your scariest dream. Feel how similar fear and excitement can be.

Affirmation: I value all that I am and all that I have. I live in peace!

WEEK 15

The problem is not the problem.
It is your current solution that is the problem.
— Reverend Yvonne Racine, Unity Church of Edmonton

Roadside Attractions: Happiness vs. Indulgence

I have noticed that there are three kinds of people: ones who save, ones who spend, and ones who balance both. The third type are the ones who have the greatest opportunity to truly reach the destination of their choice.

Are you a Spender or a Saver? Why?

_____

_____

_____

_____

_____

_____

_____

_____

Savers

Why do people do what they do with money? Often, savers are envied for their wealth, but are they truly wealthy? Not necessarily. Far too often, I meet retired people who saved all their lives, but can't stop now. They worked hard for their money and saved it for a rainy day, but they cannot enjoy their money and are still poor in their own minds. They are using their money to buy security. No amount of money will ever make you secure.

I once met a man of about 68 years of age. He was very frugal. He lived only on his monthly pension and old age security payments from the government. If he needed extra money, he rented out his basement. All of his friends felt sorry for him. They ended up buying him a new car so that it would be easier for him to get around town. Now, I know that this man had over $500,000 in investments. He had money, but could not spend it because he had not released the fear that prompted him to save it in the first place. When I asked him how much money he needed to feel that he had enough, he did not know the answer. More money is never the answer to your money problems. There is never enough money to assuage your fear.

Spenders

Spenders have their own issues. They are using money to buy something too. It is just not what they think it is. Let's take a look at where you spend your disposable cash.

What are the biggest items that you buy that are non-essential?

_____

_____

_____

_____

What qualities or values are you trying to attain with these things? Are you buying fun with the family, or are you buying your family's love? Are you buying beautiful things for the house because you value beauty, or are you buying your friends' respect? I use my money to buy beauty, freedom, and ease. I love feeling surrounded by beauty. I value how I spend my time and consider choices that give me the freedom to travel or take personal time off work. I prefer to put my energy towards creating, not just doing or working, which makes me feel at ease and releases the stress in my life.

As you dig deeper, you will find some interesting answers. A client once admitted that she was buying distraction. She was trying to fill her inner feelings of emptiness with stuff. She was spending her money in an indulgent way so that she would not have to look at how messy her life was. Then, she could always use the excuse that she didn't have any money, and so she couldn't do what she really wanted to do, which is a victim stance. This woman made over $60,000 a year.

Whenever we feel like a victim, it is because we are sacrificing ourselves. Sacrifice happens whenever we are not following our inner voice—our deepest desires. Wherever there is sacrifice, we indulge somewhere else in our lives. Stop the sacrifice and you will naturally stop the indulgence.

Let's look at indulgences in food because this issue seems to be rampant in our society. Why do people overeat? They are trying to fill a void in their lives. They are trying to suppress feelings and emotions they would rather not face. They are trying to settle for a life that does not feed their soul.

As you open to actually focus on feeding the soul what it craves, the behaviour of using food or spending money to fill this hole is no longer needed and ceases. When people try to curb their overeating or stick to a budget without looking at the deeper issues that are driving their behaviour, they are "white knuckling" it: with hands firmly gripping the steering wheel, you try to control your actions and emotions that swirl like a snowstorm around you. As soon as you lose focus for one minute, the subconscious takes control and the eating or spending begins again. In order to heal this issue, the conscious and subconscious need to unite in purpose.

What are you really trying to buy? What need are you trying to fulfill with indulgent spending?

_____

_____

_____

_____

It's important to identify the underlying need to be able to change the behaviour. I have heard it called the "latte factor." We spend little bits of money on things that add very little value to our lives, instead of choosing what truly makes us happy. Another client of mine went to great lengths to explain why he could not afford to add to his retirement account. At the time, I knew that he and his wife were spending $5 each per day at Starbucks. $5 x 2 x 30 = $300 per month. I asked him whether he wanted to retire at 60 or 65. He said 60. I replied "Great, all you have to do to stop buying coffee each morning." He shook his head and grunted about its being one of his only pleasures of the day. How sad is that? Then I asked, "Are you willing to put in another five years of your life at a job that you have said does not satisfy you, just to have a morning coffee?" Put in those terms, when he became conscious of the choice he was making, he started to save $300 a month and is well on his way to retirement at 60.

All of us make choices each and every day about what is important to us. As we bring consciousness to the consequences of these choices, our values become crystal clear. When I first began my financial plan at 29, I asked myself. "Do I want _____ (whatever it was) or do I want to retire?" I never had a sense of sacrifice or doing without because I was going for what was truly the most important thing to me.

As reported from Statistics Canada for 2004:

Percentage of eligible RSP room used: 8%
Percentage of eligible tax filers who contribute: 30%
Canadian median annual contribution: $2,600

Here is how fast things are changing. On December 21st, 2005, Mark Brown reported in the *Advisor's Edge*, "This year (2005) most Canadians estimate they will need nearly $900,000 saved up to retire, that's up from $731,000 in 2004 and markedly higher than the $530,000 in 2003." How is a $2,600 median RSP annual contribution going to accomplish this?

I become excited working with people on their financial plans. With a financial plan, you will only have to save enough money to do what you truly want to do, and then you can freely spend the rest without any guilt.

One of the most commonly cited reasons for divorce is money. Of course it is not actually about the money, it is about the inability of two people to reach a satisfactory balance in their money issues. A saver is very likely to marry a spender. I love how the universe brings us together to learn about balance.

There is never enough money to buy the security a saver needs, and never enough money for the spender to spend. They are at war about getting their needs met. When they choose to sit down with me, we draw up a financial plan that will ensure that both parties' needs are met. There will be enough money for the saver to feel safe and then they can freely spend the rest of the money. Isn't your marriage worth a financial plan? Isn't your life?

While at first glance it may seem that the saver is the sacrificer and the spender the indulger, the truth is that they are both indulging in opposite behaviours to compensate for the fact that neither of them is truly going towards their dream destination. How much money will your dream cost? That depends on how you want to travel. It is all up to you.

This week look at one of your goals that requires financing. Make some concrete plans about how you will finance it. Ensure that you continue spending 15 minutes on this project each day. As you complete the plan for one dream, work on another. For example, let's say you want to renovate your home. Will you decide on how much the overall job will be and then set up a savings plan to accumulate that amount? Include an amount to allow for rising costs, budget overruns, etc. Or, break the total renovation down into smaller pieces—maybe you will put in new plumbing this year, new flooring the next, paint the following year, etc. How much will you budget for each of those projects and where will the money come from to finance the project?

Affirmation: I choose to be happy!
I have all the money I need
to have everything I want.

WEEK 16
Your Travel Consultant: A Financial Planner

If you think you don't need a financial planner, think again. No matter how much money or financial knowledge you have, you need a financial planner. Even if you are a financial planner yourself, get someone else to work with.

In addition to being an investment advisor, it is a financial planner's responsibility to keep up to date on all income tax regulations, and that is where a lot of money can really be saved. Estate planning lawyers are surprised to find that, as a financial planner, I know more about estate planning, tax, and investment strategies than most accountants.

Notice that I am suggesting you work with a financial planner, not just an investment advisor, and not just a broker. Focusing only on your most recent investment returns will get you into trouble. It would be like buying a vehicle without first considering its purpose. A plush interior may look good, but is of no value if the primary use of the vehicle is for hauling dirt. The plush interior may be a nice bonus if you have already chosen the vehicle that has the most strength, but the interior should never be the deciding factor of what you are going to buy. Trust me when I say that investments are often dressed up with a plush appearance. Appearances can be deceiving: be clear on what you are going to use your investments for.

Unfortunately, no one can see into the future. No one can guarantee you the next hot investment. If they could, why would they be working? If they could, they would be managing their own fortune. We can look at trends and make appropriate suggestions, but no one is accurate 100% of the time. Investors are tempted to judge based on the most recent performance. That is the same as driving in the rear-view mirror. Turn that car around!

You want to work with someone who understands your dreams and goals. You want someone who is working with you on your life plan. You want to work with someone who will help you get where you would rather be. Hopefully, by now, you are convinced that whether you are looking at your life, your relationships, your money, or your goals, you need a plan. You'll get that with a financial planner!

Have someone on your team who can help you make a sound financial plan to ensure that you get there. Also, ensure that they make the kind of investments you prefer working with, so that you can continue investing with your planner throughout the years. Planning is not a single event. As your life changes, so does your plan.

People who work with financial planners get better results because planners help you manage your emotions. I began my career at the end of 1999. Things were great. People could not throw enough money into the markets. The tech sector was getting returns of over 100% in one year. During that time, a disgruntled client came into our office, complaining that his return was only 89% and he knew of another fund that got 120%. My colleague tried to talk to him about his risk tolerance, his dreams, and his goals. The client did not listen.

The year 2000 hit. The tech sector hit the skids. Over the next three years, we suffered some of the worst markets in almost 120 years. Interestingly enough, previously greedy investors became fearful clients during that time. Guaranteed Investment Certificates, returning a paltry 2-4.5%, were in high demand again. It looked better than the 40% loss the markets took. They looked good in the short term. Investors who sold out their equity holdings locked in their losses. Having settled for the 2-4.5%, they were not in the Canadian stock market when it returned over 26% in 2003, 14% in 2004, and 24% in 2005. All of a sudden, the GIC's didn't look so good. Again, rear-view driving investors flocked into the equity markets, this time going after oil and gas stocks as they reached all time highs. And so the pattern continues.

No one knows where the top of the market will be and no one knows where the bottom will be either. Your financial planner's job is to coach you through the times when you are tempted to think short-term about your long-term goals. Work with someone you trust and learn to understand your tolerance for various investment risks. The only reason your risk tolerance should change is if your life circumstances change. Your risk tolerance should never fluctuate with the markets. Your financial planner's duty is to manage the human emotions of fear and greed so as not to allow them to dictate your investment decisions.

What is your role in working with a planner? Once you have worked with someone and have the financial plan to support your dreams, you must do what you said you would do to achieve the results you expect. Remember integrity? Follow the plan. No matter what amount you said you would invest each year, do it. I don't care if a better looking investment comes along. I don't care if your house needs a new roof. I don't care if the economy is in the toilet. Keeping your commitment to your financial plan is really about keeping a commitment to yourself. It is keeping a commitment to be where you would rather be.

Also, keep your financial planner well advised of what is going on in all areas of your life. They can often see opportunities and vulnerabilities you would miss. I once was chatting with clients when I heard that they wanted to buy a piece of vacation property on Prince Edward Island. They had just done major renovations to their home and were already carrying more debt than they were comfortable with. Their solution was to cash in $40,000 of their investments (while the markets were down). I didn't think it was such a great idea. As I remember, we had an uncomfortable discussion. I knew that there had to be a better way. Then it dawned on me. I knew that the vacation property had been on the market for a long time, and that the high summer season was over. I suggested that they put the offer in on the property with a closing date six months later. My clients' busy season was coming up and I knew they would have the $40,000 saved in six months. They didn't think the seller would go for it and were still arguing with me about cashing in the investments. It turned out that the seller did accept the lengthy closing date, my clients did have the $40,000 for the down payment after six months, they did not incur any interest or redemption costs, and the investments that they had wanted to sell went up 10% in that time. This is why you should be in regular contact with your planner. They work with money issues every day and have more ideas than you can imagine. Make them your money management partner.

If you are unhappy or concerned about something involving your financial planner, tell them first. Like any good partnership, communication is absolutely required.

If you are happy with your planner, refer them to your friends, family, co-workers, and the others in your life. People are often looking for financial advice, but don't talk about it. People would rather talk about their sex lives than their finances. Referring your planner will make you a highly valued client. As you help build their business they will want to take even better care of you, and the person you referred will be grateful to you.

Work with only one financial planner, one that you trust and that you will listen to. Having multiple planners or financial advisors is like having several car mechanics. How does having several mechanics work? Would you take your car in for oil changes at both places, wasting their time and your money? If one mechanic was looking after the engine and another was for looking after the brakes, who would be looking out for the exhaust system? If you used mostly one mechanic to do the work, but the other for a second opinion, how long would the second mechanic keep investing his time with no return? Can you see that it just doesn't make sense? Working with multiple financial planners is like trying to take two different routes to the same location. Work as a partner with your financial planner, and get all your investments headed in the same direction.

Do you trust yourself? Do you trust yourself to choose the best planner for you? Do you trust yourself to choose the correct course of action? Do you trust yourself to read the road signs? You see, I am not talking about handing over everything to your financial coach. That would be creating a dependent relationship. You should have enough financial knowledge to detect when things are on or off course. For example, I have no knowledge of car mechanics, which always leaves me wary of a new mechanic. I don't trust the garage because I do not trust my own knowledge of mechanics. I could choose to totally trust my new mechanic and do all the repairs suggested, but would I be paying too much? This decision will create a constant state of mistrust and fear every time I go to the shop. On the other hand, I could get some basic education on the subject myself. Having some information, and working in partnership with my mechanic would allow me to ask smart questions and understand his answers.

Another reason for educating yourself is that what you focus on increases. Learn something about money. It will increase your awareness and increase your trust in yourself and in your financial coach. Your financial planner is an excellent source for relevant information. There is a lot of information out there, but it is not all for the vision you want to create. Be a partner, not a sideliner when it comes to your money—and your life.

This week, continue journalling for 15 minutes a day in your Road Log. If you do not have a financial planner, ask for referrals and set up appointments to meet with each one. Don't make your choice until you have met with all the candidates. Keep notes on each meeting and remember that we all have a tendency to pick the last person we met with because they are fresh in our minds. Use your notes to keep yourself objective and feel free to set up second appointments if you are not sure. You can ask each planner for their ideas of what might work in your case. Remember that you are choosing a lifelong consultant, so don't rush. Your goal should be to establish a partnership with a financial planner within the next month.

If you are already working with a financial planner, you can start from here. Meet with your planner and review all of your goals. There should be plans in place for each of your dreams. Once all the plans are agreed upon (that's partnership, again), then commit to the plans and make keeping your commitments as easy as possible (eg. automated contributions on a monthly basis). After discussion with your financial planner, agree on how many meetings you will have each year, and set up the next appointment. At your meetings, focus on how well you are meeting your goals and objectives (not the latest high flying investment you've heard of from Uncle Lou).

**Affirmation: I choose to be happy!
I'm becoming a financial wizard.**

WEEK 17
Travel Companions

Before we get started this week, how or what you are feeling?

_____

_____

_____

Think of something or someone or some situation that is currently irritating you or is still unresolved from the past. Write a few details about it.

_____

_____

_____

_____

_____

_____

_____

List ten things that annoy you e.g. war, taxes, the government, your in-laws, your boss.

_____

_____

_____

_____

_____

_____

_____

Now, how do you feel? Better or worse than when you first started?

_____

_____

_____

_____

Likely, you are not feeling as good as when you started. Sorry about that, but I wanted to prove a point. Comedian and actor Buddy Hackett once said, "I've had a few arguments with people, but I never carry a grudge. You know why? While you're carrying a grudge, they're out dancing." Complaining makes you feel bad. It puts negative energy out into the world and then that same energy comes back to you. That's what your mother meant when she told you: "What goes around, comes around." Sharing our complaints also makes others feel worse. As we share the complaint, we lower our personal vibration, dump our negative energy on our friends, and lower their vibration also. So why do we do it? What's the payoff?

All people have challenges and difficult times in their

lives. They need to talk and be supported. Sometimes it hurts. Sharing pain is not something shameful. It is often the first step in acknowledging that something needs to change and is the first step in healing.

Unfortunately, some people get stuck in the whining, bitching, and complaining phase. The root of a complaint is an unresolved issue. Complainers resist taking responsibility for their situation, they feel powerless, are stuck in the victim stance, and are looking to others for confirmation and validation that they are right.

Whatever you complain about immediately becomes more powerful than you.
— Christopher Moon, author and workshop facilitator

Faced with the choice: "Would you rather be right or happy?" complainers have not chosen happiness. Whenever you choose to be right, there must be someone or something that is wrong: If you are not wrong, you don't need to change, and it's no longer your fault or responsibility, right? Can you see how a resistance to change can actually create a feeling of powerlessness? The problem occurs when we think it is someone or something else that needs to change. Trying to get someone else to change is just another way that we keep ourselves stuck. *You* need to change. You are the only answer to your problems. You are the only saviour you have.

At another level, the releasing of energy through constantly complaining about a situation makes the problem more bearable. As issues remain unresolved, there is a natural build up of emotions and energy. This energy can help move you forward. It is energy meant to support your needed change. When we are stuck and don't use the energy for change, those pent up emotions need to be released.

Some people let off steam with angry attacks. Some release that energy on their friends by sharing their tales of woe. For those who have seen this pattern, you know that you can feel dumped on—because you have been. Your friend has dumped their pent up negative energy on you and lowered your vibration. A lower vibration weakens your personal power. It feels draining because it is. However, your friend feels much better because they have released their pent up energy on you. This is how the victim becomes the victimizer. In the balance of life, you cannot be one without being the other, in some way.

Another benefit for the drama king or queen is the amount of attention they get through having the very best "how awful" stories. We all need attention, but some people are addicted to it. No matter how much attention they get, it never fills their empty well. They are the "Enough about me. It's your turn. What do you think about me?" types. You often feel robbed in their company, because you have been. When we give someone our attention, we are also giving them some of our energy. In a balanced and healthy exchange, we take turns giving and receiving energy. We feel closer to one another. In a one-sided exchange, the giver is drained and does not get renewed. Of course, afterward, the drama addict always feels much better.

Now, almost everyone has something they want to improve in their life. The difference lies in their strategy. Ever notice how uncomfortable it is to drive in reverse? Your neck is twisted, your eyes are darting to every mirror, and you are moving slowly. When people are whining, bitching, or complaining, they are focused in the rear-view mirror. They re-experience the same roads they have driven over before.

As long as you focus on the past, you bring the situation into the present, and it becomes your future. You are talking about what has already happened, instead of focusing on what you really want to create in you life. Instead of seeing how much you have to be grateful for, you are looking at the problems.

I have already mentioned a few ideas as to why that cycle continues. There could also be deeply buried heartbreaks in your subconscious that drive this behaviour, but they are beyond the scope of this book, as you probably require skilled support or professional help to bring these up to consciousness where they can then be healed.

If you want something to change in life, you have to change direction. You must be willing to take responsibility for your choices. You have to start focusing and driving the car forward. This involves changing your point of focus. As you focus on what you want to create, you bring that future into your present.

The field of quantum physics explains vibration and frequency. You create more of what you focus on because you are always attracting people, events, and things that match your vibration. This is what the saying: "Birds of a feather flock together" means. So, if you are happy and excited about life, you will attract what maintains your happiness and excitement. The higher your vibration, the stronger your personal power for good. You become more intelligent, resourceful, and creative.

If you are angry or depressed, you will attract what maintains your anger or depression. Your lowered vibration keeps you weakened and this feeling of powerlessness continues the cycle. Focusing on what you want out of life makes you excited and raises your personal vibration. Focusing on what you don't want creates negativity and lowers your personal vibration. The same simple principle applies whether you are positively or negatively focused. You attract more of what you are focused on.

For example, let's look at a goal of losing weight. If you are focused on what the scale is saying today and are feeling bad about it, or cursing your fat belly and thighs, you will often get more results that make you feel bad, fat, and ugly. You draw in your energy and your light fades as your vibration is lowered. If instead you focus on the beauty that is already there, with true appreciation and gratitude, and you can see the flat belly and the trim thighs before they arrive, you will raise your vibration. Your happiness will attract more that makes you happy. This is the only technique that has ever been effective in supporting me to lose weight.

Personally, I want to spend as much time as possible with people who laugh and encourage me to keep growing. I want to spend time with people who praise me, but who will also tell me the truth when I'm stuck. Notice the word praise. P-raise. It raises us up to become more than we thought possible. It raises our vibration! As our vibration rises, so does our personal power. We become stronger inside. People who share their good news uplift you and fill you with inspiration. If you are not one already, you can become one of those people. Be a true light in the world.

Who is travelling this journey of life with you? Have you filled your life with those who nurture, support, and raise you? Or, are you the person who does the nurturing, supporting, and propping up without getting much back in return? How is the balance in your life? How well is it working for you?

_____

_____

_____

_____

_____

_____

_____

Here is an interesting exercise to try with anyone who is stuck. Ask them what they want, then what they are going to do about it. Their answers should be enlightening. I was once having dinner with a friend and her co-worker stopped by to update her on the latest transgression of their supervisors. I asked him what he wanted to see happen. I also asked him what he had tried to do to create change. He explained that he had stopped trying because it had not gotten him the results he wanted. I then asked him if complaining to others had gotten him the results he wanted. He quickly left the table, which was the result I wanted!

You may think that I was being cruel to this young fellow, but allowing others to continue in the direction of complaining disempowers them and is not a loving approach. Constant complainers drain energy from others because they are not creating positive energy for themselves. We always have a choice to give our energy to something that raises us up or pulls us down.

The above questions are important because becoming aware is the fastest way to get back in the right direction. You will encounter disappointment and disillusionment along the way, but extended complaining is not going to help. I have a three time rule of thumb. I allow myself to whine about a single subject three times. It is important to acknowledge any issue and release the pain attached. After three times, I know that I am resisting getting the message. So I ask myself, "What do I want?" and "What can I do to change this?" I learn the lesson. I take action. I'm back in the driver's seat, headed in the right direction!

Anger is energy against...
Passion is energy for...

Anger makes you a victim.
Passion makes you a creator!

What is your current complaint? Who or what is bothering you?

_____

_____

_____

_____

What do you want from this situation that you are currently not getting?

_____

_____

_____

_____

What does the other person need?

_____

_____

_____

_____

_____

_____

_____

How can you change to improve the situation? How can you become a leader here? What can you do to ensue that both parties' needs are being met equally?

_____

_____

_____

_____

What is the lesson?

_____

_____

_____

_____

I know a woman who has trouble taking full responsibility for her future because she does not want to take responsibility for what she created in the past. She has confused responsibility with blame. She is so busy beating herself up that she will not put energy into looking forward. She is still looking in the rear-view mirror.

The past is the past, and you did the best you could with the skills you had in the past. If you could have done better, you would have. Beating ourselves up is just another form of holding ourselves back. Stop it. It does not work. You need kind and loving and supportive messages. And you must give them to yourself daily.

To have a truly happy and fulfilled life, you need to surround yourself with people who raise your energy and vibration, and you need be the kind of person who does the same for others.

What are the qualities that make you want to be with a person?

_____

_____

_____

_____

_____

_____

_____

_____

Make a list of the 15 people that you spend the most time with down the left hand side of the page.

_____	_____	_____
_____	_____	_____
_____	_____	_____
_____	_____	_____
_____	_____	_____
_____	_____	_____
_____	_____	_____
_____	_____	_____
_____	_____	_____
_____	_____	_____
_____	_____	_____
_____	_____	_____
_____	_____	_____
_____	_____	_____
_____	_____	_____

Down the middle of the columns, number your friends, co-workers, and family in the order of your preference.

After you've done that, write out the four or five qualities that describe each person, in the right-hand column. These are the qualities that you admire and uplift you. What have you learned from this?

_____

_____

_____

_____

_____

_____

Are there any qualities that you would like to further develop in your own personality?

_____

_____

_____

Let's look at the bottom #11-15 people on your list. Write out four or five qualities that you don't you like about each.

_____

_____

_____

_____

_____

Are you aware of any trends emerging? What about these qualities is distasteful or threatening to you?

_____

_____

_____

_____

_____

_____

_____

Why do you have these people in your life? What could you learn from them?

_____

_____

_____

_____

_____

_____

_____

Do you want to do anything about it? You can accept them and your relationship as it is. You can talk to them about what bothers you. You can stop spending time with them. You could do an **Integration Process for Dilemmas and Conflicts** (see Tool Box) of their perceived weakness with your perceived strength. What other choices do you want to make? Remember: do it, dump it, date it, or delegate it.

_____

_____

_____

_____

_____

_____

_____

Do you have any of those same qualities that you dislike in others? Have you ever acted in that way? Are you judging yourself about it? Is forgiveness needed?

_____

_____

_____

_____

_____

_____

This week I ask you to go out and have some fun with people you truly enjoy. Each day, consider how your time was spent and what you liked or didn't like about each social engagement. Is there anything new you would like to create in your life after reflecting upon the people you spend time with?

Affirmation: I choose to be happy! My joy, laughter, and happiness are the magnets that attract like-minded people into my life.

WEEK 18
Your Battery

A battery with only one pole doesn't work. A person who views life with only one perspective—whether it's positive or negative—is blind.
— Christopher Moon, author and workshop facilitator

How are things going? Has your experience of working with a cheerleader or Master Mind Group gone well? Where are you currently feeling challenged? Are you taking time to rest and enjoy life? How are you celebrating your achievements? How are things proceeding financially? What are you learning? How are your partnerships? How does your vibration feel?

_____

_____

_____

_____

_____

_____

_____

_____

_____

_____

_____

_____

In his book *Real Wealth: Creating the Life You Deserve*, Phillip Smedstad ponders Albert Einstein's question: "Is this a friendly Universe?" This question hit me like a lead balloon. Here I had been going along thinking that I was a fairly positive person. I thought that I *did* believe good things would continue to be brought into my life. I thought I trusted God. But, I suddenly realized that deep in my unconscious mind, I was cultivating fearful thoughts. I was preparing for the worst possible outcome. I was on guard and had to have my weapons ready. I could never fully relax. Consciously I was thinking positively, but my unconscious personal feelings and talk were negative and fearful.

Reading Smedstad's book helped me see where I was still hanging on to catastrophic beliefs. Catastrophic beliefs arise when you are always expecting the worst and never fully receive the blessings of the present moment. I once worked for a man who demonstrated this perfectly. When the business was going through hard times, we had to pull in, save our resources, and try to do more with less, because there was less money. When business was booming, we had to pull in, save our resources, and try to do more with less, because hard times were coming again. And he had proof that he was right, because business always has cycles. I see this every day in the stock market. Whether people believe the market is going up or going down, they get to be right at some time. The point is, over time, the market has always gone up.

Preparing for the worst all the time is like saying that you can't enjoy the lake in the summer because winter is coming. Yes, winter is coming, but if you don't take time to relax, have fun, and enjoy summertime at the lake, why bother living? As you know, I believe in being prepared, but not overly prepared. I believe in having fun and knowing that indulgence will not be fun in the end. Even indulging in work eventually becomes counterproductive. I fully believe in balance.

I hope that as you look at your life, you can see that it has improved. If it has not, let me explain why. You are not driving in the direction you want to go. When we believe that the world is a treacherous place, we are on guard. We live in fear. The problem with this is that fear attracts what you fear. Not only that, it's a downward spiral. Fear keeps us stuck and then we become more fearful.

A good friend of mine believes that a romantic relationship is the source of all good things. When he is not in a relationship, he whines about not having one. When he is in one, he worries that it's going to be over. So he moves from relationship to relationship, never allowing himself to be happy. He always feels like a failure and is tied into a loop of catastrophic thinking. And that is what he continues to create.

A few years ago, I found myself encountering increasing amounts of fear. To counteract the mounting fear, I chose to deal with it head on. I was on vacation at the time and I looked for the most fear-invoking activity I could find. I went on a "Canopy Tour." I got in a harness and attached myself to a single line. I then let go and traversed from tree to tree—80 feet in the air—18 times! I was terrified.

But it worked. I faced the greatest fear in the moment and all the other minuscule fears were gone too. You see fear is a moving target. If you try to stay away from it, it moves towards you. If you retreat further, it chases you. Your world becomes smaller. It is only in facing your fears that you can expand your experience of life, raise your vibration, and increase your personal power. Jesus said:

Have faith in God. I tell you this: if anyone says to this mountain, "Be lifted from your place and hurled into the sea," and has no inward doubts, but believes what he says is happening, it will be done for him. I tell you, then, whatever you ask for in prayer, believe that you have received it and it will be yours.
— Mark 11:23, New English Bible

If you fear that things will get worse, rest assured you are right. If you believe that things are getting better, rest assured you are right.

Which belief empowers you to move forward in your life?

_____

_____

_____

_____

_____

_____

The lesson of my success in the high trees came from stepping directly into fear and trusting that I was going to be safe. I know of a famous public speaker who gets excited when a speaking engagement gets cancelled. He knows that when that happens, it is just to create space for something even bigger and more lucrative to appear. He says, "When one door closes, a better one opens."

If you knew that your road trip would be fraught with breakdowns, bad roads, poor food, and speeding tickets, you probably wouldn't leave home. But we go on vacations because we expect to have a good time.

Is the world (God, the universe) for you, or against you?_____

Is your life journey a fun adventure or a pending disaster?

_____

Are you on optimist or a pessimist?

_____

Your answers to these questions will set the stage for your results. In truth, we get to decide if what happens to us is for or against us. There is an old story about a farmer: one day his stallion broke out of the barn and ran away. The people of the town said "That's too bad." He replied that it could be a bad thing or a good thing. Days later the stallion returned with a harem of young mares behind him. The town's people said "That's a great thing." The farmer replied that it could be a good thing or a bad thing. The farmer's son got busy breaking and training the new horses for market. Unfortunately, a horse kicked him and broke his leg. Again, the town's folk said "That is a horrible thing to happen to your son." The farmer stood firm in his response: "It could be a horrible thing, or it could be a good thing." The following month, the army came through town and conscripted all the young men of the village. Because of his broken leg, the farmer's son did not have to go fight in the war. Was it a good thing or a bad thing?

Notice that I am not saying that everything will be wonderful once you set out on the journey. The one drawback of purely positive, or Pollyanna, thinking is that life will broadside you. There are always new lessons to be learned.

Pollyanna thinking also occurs when you are not grounding your life energy. I am not going to go into depth about this as there are many great books, studies, and healing arts that deal with the subject of grounding, but here is a simple, effective exercise to explore.

Grounding Exercise

All that you need to do to ground your energy is to imagine (as you work with this more, you will eventually be able to feel) the energy coming from the earth and entering your body from the middle of your feet. Imagine and feel that energy coming up through your legs, filling your body, arms, and head. Then visualize the energy leaving through the top of your head. Now reverse that, see universal energy coming into the top of your head, travelling through and filling your body, and exiting out the bottom of your feet. There are many different techniques for grounding, but this is a quick one that works for me. Grounding helps stop the thoughts that take your attention from what is happening in the present moment. Grounding clears your mind of chatter and clutter. When you are fully grounded and present, you will be much more conscious of things in your surroundings, and your intuition will be enhanced. This way you are more capable of dealing with any potholes on your journey. When you can see what is coming, you are less likely to be side-swiped or have an accident.

If you are a positive optimist, a balance of preparation for another outcome will save you time, money, and frustration. If you are more of a pessimist, you are prepared for things to go wrong, so you will need to practice being more optimistic. Balance is the key.

Think of something you want to improve in your life.

_____

_____

What could you do about it?

_____

_____

_____

_____

If you are a positive person, let yourself think of one thing that could go wrong and how you would handle it. If you tend to think more negatively, let yourself think of a positive outcome and how you would feel about it.

_____

_____

_____

_____

_____

_____

If you are a positive person, let yourself think of another thing that could go wrong and how you would handle it. If you tend to think more negatively, let yourself think of another positive outcome and how you would feel about it.

_____

_____

_____

Throughout your life, many things will happen. If you be-lieve they are for your good, you will be open to receive the next great thing in your life. If you believe they are against you, you will pull in, play small, and never try again. Be-lieving in the worst will keep you stuck. I find that expecting the best and having at least one backup plan works best. When I am grounded and in balance, I feel confident and pre-pared. The funny thing is that no matter what happens, I am never fully prepared, but I trust that I can handle whatever comes along.

In goal setting, people will often start by looking at where they do not want to go instead of what they do want. Look at your motivation. Are you running away from something you don't like, or focused on creating your heart's desire? It can seem like a small difference, but it is a major one. When you are trying to run away from something, you are filled with fear and anger. When you are moving towards what you want, you are filled with passion and excitement. One is a low vibration, the other a high vibration. Both are emotions and emotions create.

As we are running away from something, we are still fo-cusing on it. It is like the issue is chasing us. As you've heard me say many times, what we focus on expands. We simply get more of it. People have the hardest time making change happen when they are running away. It will not happen as long as we are still driving while looking in the rear-view mirror. You must let go of whatever you want to run away from. True letting go can only be done with gratitude and ap-preciation.

Let's say that you want to be worth a million dollars, but

each day you are still fussing and fuming about about how you will pay the bills. You are giving your attention and energy to the bills, not the million dollars. You are focused on survival. And, what you give your attention and energy to grows. Try this instead.

Instead of viewing your bills with dread, look at them as a blessing. That you have received a bill is proof that someone believes that you can pay it. Keep blessing that bill and the people who believe in you, until you have the money to pay it. If you have an electrical bill, see the blessing that electricity is to your life. A mortgage payment allows you to appreciate the shelter of your home. The dentist bill is for your healthy teeth. See how different it feels? Shift from dread to gratitude. It will make all the difference to your energy for life. From gratitude, it is much easier to take responsibility and see new choices. You will see that you are able to create money. If you can create *some* money, then you can create a lot more of it. Keep focused on blessings and gratitude.

Gratitude List

Oprah Winfrey has been a staunch promoter of gratitude journals. Some recommend starting each day with a list of ten things you are grateful for. Try it!

I am grateful for:

_____

_____

_____

_____

_____

_____

_____

_____

_____

_____

Doesn't that feel fabulous?

As you know, I am (and I hope you are too) a believer in the importance of starting your day with some form of reflective writing. It only takes a few minutes to help create a wonderful day.

About 20 years ago, I took a trip to northern Brazil. I had won one round trip to anywhere in the world that Canadian Airlines flew. I chose the farthest destination that had a Club Med. Because I was travelling alone, I wanted a resort style that I was familiar with so that I wouldn't have any surprises. I also wanted a place that people came to as a destination, so that I could get to know them. Well, I arrived for a two-week vacation, only to find that almost no one spoke English. Thank goodness the bartender spoke seven languages, and he interpreted for everyone. It was a very international club. There were French, German, Portuguese, Spanish, Italian and even Russian tourists, but only two people spoke English very well. Imagine my shock and terror on the first day of arrival. I decided to make the best of it. Today, I cherish that holiday because I learned so much. The most important thing I learned was hugging. My family had not been very physically demonstrative and I fell in love with being hugged with every greeting. Even though we could not speak to each other, we felt fond affection for each other. I made a commitment to continue the practice on my return to Canada.

Now, that was over 20 years ago and hugging was not the common practice that it is today. At first people were a little uncomfortable, but I kept my commitment. After three or four hugs, people started to relax and accept it. And now, they stand with open arms. John Kanary, a famous international motivation speaker says: "We need ten hugs a day, just to stay healthy," and I agree with him.

Not only did I learn the importance of body language in Brazil, I also learned the importance of "programming" myself. Each night, we would all meet at the bar before dinner. I didn't know what the other guests were saying to me, but I just answered in gibberish and then we would all laugh. One night, a gentleman asked me, using sign language, why I had such a long face. I didn't feel any sadness. Then it hit me: I had not "programmed" myself that evening.

You see, most nights, before heading to the bar, I stood in front of the mirror and said things to myself (the things you will do when travelling alone) such as: "I'm going to have a fabulous night." "Everyone is going to love me." "We are going to laugh all night," and other variations on the same theme. On the night I had forgotten to "program," people saw me differently. Just to make sure, I ran a little experiment with monitoring the results of nights that I programmed myself, or not. One-hundred per cent of the time, people I did not know and who I could not speak to knew the difference. That is the power of starting your day on a positive note. I was not trying to run away from my situation. I embraced it and set out to create what I wanted each night. That's personal power.

A lot of motivational speakers, workshop facilitators, and even authors tend to ask you to follow their path to happiness. I have tried many paths, but life kept "biting me in the ass." I used to think that something was wrong with me. Maybe I was doing something wrong. Horsefeathers!

Just as there are cycles in nature, life will always keep moving. There will be ups and downs in the process and you will like some things and not others. As they say about downhill skiing: "If you don't fall down every once in a while, you are not improving your abilities." There's no need to be disappointed or disillusioned. Throughout this road map process I encourage you to stop running, face things the way they are, and create a journey to where you would rather be.

This week, try this: go on a negative thought diet. Do not let yourself hold a negative thought for longer than ten seconds. Let it go. Change your focus. Even the first day will give you amazing insight into your thoughts. Write about it in your daily 15 minutes of reflective journalling.

Affirmation: I live in perfect balance, grateful for all that I have, all that I do, and all that I am.

WEEK 19
Who's at the Wheel?

When you go on vacation, how do you decide where to go? Is your choice limited by available money? Do you go along with where your travel companion wants to go? Or, do you set the agenda and ask someone else to go with you on your trip? Do you ask someone who also wants to go to that same location?

_____

_____

_____

_____

_____

_____

_____

_____

_____

_____

_____

I have found that the way in which you do one thing is the way you usually do everything. If you are not living in peace and harmony, something is not working. And when things are not working, you are not getting where you want to go.

Let's look at how you handle your life.

Who picks the movie? _____

What happens when you and your companion don't want to see the same movie?

_____

_____

_____

_____

_____

_____

_____

Who decides how to handle the money?

_____

What happens when you and your partner disagree on a purchase? An investment? Budgeting?

_____

_____

_____

_____

_____

_____

_____

Do you get your way in most decisions? Or, do you do what the other wants to do in most cases? What is the balance in your life?

_____

_____

_____

_____

_____

_____

_____

_____

_____

There are no right or wrong answers here, but are you seeing a pattern?

Life is meant to be a shared journey. In fact, you cannot do it alone. We need each other in so many ways. When we usually insist that others do what we want, or when we usually do what the other person wants, there is an underlying struggle for power. If you always have to have things your own way, you want control. If you are always acquiescing to another's desires, you want acceptance and approval and you give your power away in exchange. Both approaches are serious obstacles to your journey. When you are in any kind of power struggle, you are at a dead stop. The competition and need gratification have become more important than your partner. To move forward, you must balance your needs with the needs of others. You must invest the time and energy to play a win/win game in your life. You must acknowledge that we are all truly interdependent. You give and you receive.

OK. I can hear some of you now. "That only works if the

other person is playing a win/win game, too." In my past I tried to play win/win, but just ended up playing you win/I lose. You can imagine that I wasn't too thrilled with a prolonged experience of that game. It seemed that as I struggled to trust others, I kept producing unsatisfactory results. There was an error in my process.

I had been whining to a workmate about someone I said I couldn't trust. She responded that she trusted him fully— she trusted him to make the politically correct decision. She was right. I had wanted him to make the decisions that I thought were best for me. Oops, that was dependency! I had given him part of my power and part of my responsibility. It was up to me to make decisions for me. I had to take care of myself. Certainly he would make some decisions that would benefit me, but it was up to me to ensure that I spoke up against decisions that did not feel right to me.

I see this so often with people and their physicians. They take whatever the doctor says as gospel truth, even if it does not feel right to them, sometimes to their own detriment. Relationships are meant to be partnerships, not co-dependent facsimiles of a parent/child interaction. Just because your car is on cruise control, you can't fall asleep. You have to stay awake and that means staying conscious and fully engaged. Whenever you don't listen to inner guidance, you have given your power over to some one else. Don't do it. Stand up for your truth. Once you start trusting yourself to take care of yourself, trusting others is never an issue.

You can usually trust someone to make decisions that are in their own best interest (even if it doesn't look that way to you). You need to learn to trust that you are making decisions that are best for you. If you do not agree with someone, that's when the communication really begins. Do not give in to others because it seems easier (going with the flow) or because you want to be liked. Don't sit back and do everything your partner wants. Likewise, don't sit smugly back while your partner does everything you want. Both approaches will sabotage all that you truly want to create—your heart's desires.

The long-term pain of sacrifice (giving to get something in return) is excruciating. Comedian Bill Cosby said: "I don't know the key to success, but the key to failure is to try to please everyone." Sacrifice is a strategy that always demands repayment in some way. The longer it takes for repayment, the bigger the interest due. You need to go inside yourself and check what your truth is. Share your truth and come to an agreement on what you both wholeheartedly want. When you can express this, your interaction will be loving.

In the end, conflict resolution can never truly be avoided. So, face things as soon as possible. Work together to find an answer that works for both of you. Most often, the two of you will come up with several ideas that are even better than the ones you had individually. Sometimes that answer does involve a parting of the ways, but that is sometimes the best solution and the natural development of any relationship.

One of the potholes I have fallen into is thinking that I knew what the winning solution would be for the other person. Never assume (it makes an *ass* of *u* and *me*). Ask. It shows you care enough to listen.

Of course, the other pitfall I have encountered is not being clear on what the winning solution would be for me and not knowing what I truly wanted. A person would come along and ask me to do something. At the time, I would often automatically say yes, even if I felt I really didn't want to do it. I would think thoughts like: "It wouldn't hurt me to do this," or "I should." Well, sometimes it did hurt me and I shouldn't have. By gaining clarity, using any method that works for you, about what you want, and by asking what the other person truly wants, a balanced solution is much easier to achieve.

Is there anything that you would like to change about how you make decisions that involve or include others?

_____

_____

_____

_____

_____

Does making that change create any feelings of fear? Any other feelings?

_____

_____

_____

_____

_____

_____

What support do you want/need to make this change? Who do you need to talk to? What are you going to do?

_____

_____

_____

_____

_____

A couple I knew demonstrated just how awful a situation can get if you aren't willing to communicate and resolve conflict. Brenda had been running a Bed and Breakfast for a year and a half after her separation from Dave. He had a workshop for his business in the back of the property. Even though it had been a year and a half, they had not reached a divorce agreement. Each continued to blame and provoke the other. Relations got progressively worse. Dave came into the house and took things of value without consulting Brenda. He even tried to get the B & B closed down permanently while stealing another piece of art. A physical altercation ensued. The police were called and a judge arrived with a restraining order. This is an extreme example of what can happen when you are determined to stay stuck in your position of "being right." Things just get worse. Negative thoughts and feelings create more and more negativity. The longer an issue remains unresolved, the more energy will build for resolution, and the more bitter the fight will become.

Over time, any unresolved issue will grow. To resolve an issue, you need to communicate. Talk about what is bothering you. Together, work to find an answer that feels right to you both, in the spirit of partnership—not competition. In conflict, a defensive position is from fear. Resolve to stop the judgments that create negative energy and focus on raising the vibration surrounding the issue. For resolution, move to a creative position and stay focused on a win/win solution for both of you.

The same is true for unresolved issues within yourself. If you want to do something, but don't do it, the pressure rises within you. It creates stress in your life and everyone knows that too much stress can kill you. Do whatever is necessary to come to resolution. Use that energy to get yourself moving. You will feel so much better. It will be like a weight has been lifted off your shoulders.

What unresolved issue is between you and another?

_____

_____

_____

_____

_____

_____

_____

_____

What are you going to do about it? How can you achieve resolution?

_____

_____

_____

_____

_____

_____

_____

_____

What is it that you have wanted to do for a long time, but haven't done?

_____

_____

_____

_____

_____

_____

How are you going to resolve that desire? Remember resolution is do it, dump it, date it, or delegate it.

_____

_____

_____

_____

_____

_____

_____

Whenever you feel out of balance or unresolved, use the **Integration Exercise** (in the Tool Box) for finding energetic balance.

As you start taking care of yourself, you start to build trust in yourself and others. As trust in yourself expands, so does your ability to be more active or less active in your life (depending on in which direction balance lies for you). You can take more chances because you trust that you can handle whatever happens. The results will not always be as you expected them, but what you learn will be the very best for you and essential to your long-term success.

I love listening to interviews with famous people (stars). I have never heard one say that they became famous because they took everyone's advice or copied another performer. Over and over again, I hear, "I had to do it my way." You can choose to be a poor replica of someone else, or you can choose to be a fabulous and original *you*. No one else can play your part. Your heart calls you to play your own role.

This week, clear up at least one unresolved issue in your life. Watch how you make decisions with others and journal about your decision making process.

**Affirmation: I choose to be happy!
I always create balance
in my relationships and within myself.**

WEEK 20

One of the greatest discoveries a man makes,
one of his great surprises,
is to find he can do what he was afraid he couldn't do.
— Henry Ford, 1863-1947, founder of Ford Motor Company

Higher Power

Connecting to a source of power greater than you believe yourself to be makes everything easier and more manageable. What you call that power source—God, the Universe, your unconscious, angels, universal energy—does not matter. What *does* matter is that you learn to harness and work with the support that is always available for you. If you believe something is possible, it will work for you. If you believe you are alone and must do everything yourself, you will have to.

I have had some serious struggles with my concept of God, so I know that some of you will also have a difficult time with this section. Just be open to a short examination.

If you believe that you are alone in the universe, that will be your experience. If you believe you are being helped, that will be your experience. If you believe you are guilty, you will be punished. It does not matter what you believe; you will be able to prove it because you only see what you believe.

Can you see radio waves, television transmissions, or electricity? Your not being able to see them doesn't mean they don't exist. They are real and you have learned to believe in their existence because you have practiced turning on the switch and seeing their effect. Is this faith or fact?

Earlier in the book, I mentioned that we can choose to be surrounded by whatever raises us up or brings us down. Let's look at your beliefs about a Higher Power. Do they empower and enhance your energy, or do they limit you?

My beliefs concerning a Higher Power are:

_____

_____

_____

_____

_____

_____

_____

These beliefs empower and/or limit me by:

_____

_____

_____

_____

_____

As a child, I learned the concept of a punishing God, at least that is how my young mind interpreted things. I believed that every hardship was a punishment from God. So, I tried again and again and harder and harder to be a good girl. I thought that if I followed all the rules, God would take care of me. This is a stage of dependence. When I was very, very good and things still didn't happen as I wanted them to, I decided it was all God's fault. He had let me down. So, I dumped my belief in God and entered a stage of independence. I became completely in charge of my life. I was on my own. Unfortunately, I was also limited by how small I felt and perceived myself to be. There was no help for me, but at least I wasn't going to be disappointed again. Notice the heartbreak in this strategy? Ever do this in your personal relationships?

Fifteen years ago, I took a course called "The Pursuit of Excellence" (a perfect course name for someone trying to be good). In this course, they once again introduced me to the idea of a Higher Power. I had more than a little resistance, but what I was doing wasn't working, and I was in enough pain that I thought: "I'll just open a little bit." A few months later, I met a woman, Heather Clarke, who took me to the Centre for Positive Living. I cried the entire service. There they believed in a Power that loved me...no matter what. I could actually feel the love in the air, and I cried and my heart opened.

But I am not one to be conquered so easily. Away from the church service, my doubts and fears of further disappointment crept in. Heather challenged me to ask for "a sign" for the truth about the existence of Universal Energy, and, to ask for a sign that even I, in my distrust, would recognize.

Within two days, I heard a radio advertisement for a sale on party dresses at a downtown department store. As Christmas cocktail season was about to begin, I went over to the store on my lunch hour. The sales clerk looked at me like I was crazy. "Sales on those dresses don't start until party season is over." On my way out, in my confusion, I was attracted to a fur salon. I had never gone shopping for a fur before, but felt drawn to take a peek. On the wall, I spotted the coat. It was the only full-length beaver coat in the store. It was my size. It was 75% off!

Now what do a full-length beaver coat and higher power

have in common? My desire! My desire for a sign and my desire for a coat intersected. Six months prior, I had written down a list of grandiose goals. I had written them down, but never focused on them. I never even looked at them again. I never did anything to move towards achieving them in any conscious way—I simply forgot about them. What floored me was that a "full-length beaver coat" was on the list. I knew the coat was a sign that there was a power greater than my limited view of myself. You may not come to the same conclusion I did, but I encourage you to ask for your own sign.

I finally realized that if I had to rely only on myself, I was going to achieve very little. I saw myself as small, and in truth, I was living a very small life. Deciding that there is a source of power or universal energy (again, whatever you want to call it) that is working for you will help you understand how powerful and creative you can be.

Turning for assistance to my Higher Power has helped me in so many ways. I don't have to struggle to find solutions to my questions, fears, or problem. I ask for solutions and they are drawn to me. I know that whenever I think or feel I do not have the power, or the strength, or the ability, or the knowledge to fix a situation, I can just desire for things to be handled. Then I listen for direction—sometimes from myself, sometimes from others. When it feels right, I take action in that direction.

I set the course, focus on what I want, and trust that whatever comes into my life is brought to me for my good. Even though it may not look like it at the time, I do know that it is my Higher Power's way of moving me toward my heart's desire. I continue going inside to check for inspiration and take action on that guidance. It's always a more beautiful destination than I could ever have reached by myself.

So, whether you choose to have universal support on your

journey or not, you will have the experiences you are focused on. However connecting to your Higher Power will get you there with fewer detours, smoother roads, and more fun.

This week, complete a list of 100 goals as below. If you would like as sign from a Higher Power, just ask. You could receive a miracle. Be light about it. Remember that a lighter vibration has more power for more good.

What miracle would you like to see?

_____

_____

_____

_____

_____

_____

_____

_____

100 Yearly Goals—Using the Law of Attraction

Each New Year's Day, I start my annual list of 100 things I want. These are huge, grandiose goals. I do not have the faintest idea of how I can achieve them. I give them over to the Universe to create. It is an exercise to expand both my ability to see greater possibilities (stretch my limited thinking) and increase my ability to receive. These are goals that I just declare I am open to receiving. In truth, what I am doing is expanding my energy field—my magnetism. These are goals that I want to attract without putting in any conscious effort int.

I write them out as affirmations. I write them out as positive, elaborate statements phrased in current time. For example, when I wanted to earn $100,000 per year, I wrote "I now earn far in excess of $100,000 per year, with ease and grace." When I wanted to be a more loving person, I wrote:

"I have an open heart that allows me to bless myself and every person with gifts of love." Who do you want to be? What do you want to have? What do you want to do? Take your thoughts of being, doing, and having and turn them into grandiose, positive statements phrased as though you have already achieved them. The more emotion in these statements, the better. Emotion is the energy of attraction, so really feel it.

Write out 100 of these statements and put them away. I look at my list only about three times a year, and only for the purpose of checking off the goals that I know I have met in my life. Without any conscious effort on my part, I average between a 60-80% rate of achievement each year. I create by getting clear about what I want, and then just attracting the results I am seeking. What really happens is that I achieve all the things I have no resistance to. If there is something your heart truly wants, but it is not showing up in your life, it is because you have resistance to it. Resistance to achieving or receiving a specific result is found within our beliefs. It is because there is a part of us that either believes it's not possible, we don't deserve it, or we have conflicting desires. An example of conflicted desires is when we want to save a certain amount, but we also want to have every shiny thing that attracts our attention. If we indulge in daily accumulation of shiny things, our savings won't grow as we planned. Another example is when you want to attract a relationship: you want to live in peace, but past experiences of relationships are full of conflict. You always have what you have the least resistance to, so if your desire isn't showing up, something has to change internally to allow in your new desire. To investigate what's (not) going on, remember the "Principles of Creation" list I suggested you put on your mirror. Number 8 is about clearing up any personal beliefs that are blocking what you say you want. Look at why you might be afraid to have what you say you want. What might you be afraid of losing by having it? You may want to redo many of the exercises in this book, focusing solely on this one deep desire. *A Course in Miracles* says your task is not to seek love, but merely to seek and find all the barriers within yourself that you have built against it.

If you are struggling to complete your list of 100 desires (most people do), go back to your wants and needs lists from the beginning of this book. I keep this list handy so I can add new desires as they arise.

Just try this. Simply writing down your goals has a huge impact. If you do nothing else on a conscious level except write it down, you have moved your dreams from fantasies to goals.

Affirmation: I choose to be happy! I'm open to knowing my Highest Good.

WEEK 21
Arrival

Congratulations! You made it! By now, you have been working with this program for more than five months. I am so very impressed that you have come this far. I hope that it has been a fun, inspiring, challenging, joyful, and delightful journey. I hope that you already have far more of what you truly desire in your life. How is your money situation? Have you experienced any miracles yet? Take a few minutes to write about what this journey has meant to you.

_____

_____

_____

_____

_____

_____

_____

_____

_____

_____

_____

_____

_____

I'd love to hear about your experiences, so feel free to e-mail me at:

sheila.leonard@investorsgroup.com or berich@live.ca

It's now time to celebrate! What was the reward you promised yourself for completing this book? Now is the time to reward yourself. Remember that this was a commitment to yourself and even if it still feels like a stretch, it's one that must be carried out to preserve your personal integrity.

What was your planned reward? When and how are you going to let yourself have it?

_____

_____

_____

_____

_____

_____

In the meantime, take a day off, just for you. You have worked hard and deserve a rest. Do whatever you want. How about day at a spa? A personal retreat? A day in a hotel? Some time in nature? A round at the most expensive golf course in town? Have a maid come in for the day, or let go of cooking for the day. Ever rented a limousine for the day or a sporty convertible? Whatever it is, stretch. Do something that is extravagant and exciting, peaceful, and perfect for just you.

Your stretch may at first feel uncomfortable. Pay attention to any feelings of discomfort or appreciation and journal about them. Are you scared of spending money? I suggest that you work through your fear before actually spending money, or you may create your feared result. Do you feel insecure around people who have more money than you? Explore what you are thinking about yourself. Write new affirmations to help open your mind. Many people will tell you to use words like: I have, I am. I have found that my mind responds to these words with: "oh no, you don't," creating an inner conflict. I tend to add the word "choose" (e.g. I choose to have, I choose to be, or I am open to) and then my mind will accept it.

Expose yourself to a lifestyle that is currently out of your reach. Spend time with people who have a bigger experience of life than you currently have. Expand your mind. It lets you see what else is possible. It helps you develop the opposite of scarcity consciousness—prosperity consciousness.

In time, you will see the value of building prosperity consciousness. Stretch and see how much good you can allow into your life as a reward for your accomplishments.

Building prosperity consciousness can be done in so many ways and it doesn't have to cost a lot of money. Flip through luxury magazines. Choose a slightly more expensive restaurant. Tour art galleries. Window shop at expensive stores. Take expensive cars out for a test drive. Go on home tours or visit show homes. Just be careful not to sabotage yourself by impulse buying. Remember to follow your financial plan. You get the idea.

Some people avoid exposing themselves to what they cannot currently afford because it makes them feel inadequate, small, or lesser than what they see. Don't fall for that! Don't settle. Use prosperity consciousness building activities to give you new ideas of what is possible for you.

How would you like to start building prosperity consciousness?

_____

_____

_____

_____

_____

_____

How would you like to reward yourself for upholding your commitment to your dream destination? Remember to make it a stretch, something extravagant and exciting.

_____

_____

_____

_____

_____

_____

_____

How often will you schedule reward days?

_____

Put the dates on your calendar now. Start making plans for your next reward day.

As you have seen, some goals come easily and some you will be working on for years. If you haven't done so already, this is a good time to review your list of your original 150 wants and needs. As you know, wants and needs change and need to be updated at least once a year. If you have stuck with the program, you now have a lifelong road map to everything and anything you want in your life. You don't need to stop because the book is ending: your life isn't.

I encourage you to continue with this program, or integrate the parts that worked well for you, for the rest of your life. I trust that you have received the enormous benefits of investing time for reflection, exploration, and spending 15 minutes a day focused on your desires. If there were some exercises that you found challenging, or didn't choose to do at the time, consider revisiting them over the next three months. Keep visualizing, writing, re-writing, growing, and expanding your life experience. Life is a grand adventure.

Imagine that you are at the end of your life.

What do you want your epitaph to say?

_____

_____

What do you want your friends to say about you?

_____

_____

_____

_____

_____

_____

What do you want your spouse to say about you?

_____

_____

_____

_____

_____

_____

What do you want your children to say about you?

_____

_____

_____

_____

_____

_____

What do you want your co-workers or business partners to say about you?

_____

_____

_____

_____

_____

_____

Take some time to write out your own obituary.

_____

_____

_____

_____

_____

_____

_____

_____

_____

_____

_____

_____

_____

_____

_____

_____

Still imagining that you are at the end of your life, what do you want your purpose and contribution on earth to have been about?

_____

_____

_____

_____

_____

What are you most proud of?

_____

_____

_____

_____

_____

If this is what you want your life to be about, isn't it worth the time and effort to achieve it? What commitments can you put in place, today, to ensure the success of your life journey?

If you enjoyed this book, please give a copy to your friends. You never know the difference it can make.

Sheila Leonard holds the Certified Financial Planner designation and runs a successful practice in Calgary, Alberta, Canada, as a Financial Consultant with Investors Group Financial Services Inc. The views of Sheila Leonard in this publication are solely those of the author and she is responsible for the content of this publication. Investors Group Financial Services Inc. and its Affiliates are not responsible for and cannot accept any liability for any information in this publication.

For further information on upcoming seminars, or if you would like Sheila to facilitate a program in your area, please contact her at sheila.leonard@investorsgroup.com or berich@live.ca

TOOL BOX

Principles of Creation

1. Have a dream. Make it as wild and crazy and fabulous as you can imagine.
2. Be open to the idea of that dream or fantasy becoming a reality.
3. Be on the lookout for ways of accomplishing even small parts of your dream.
4. Support comes in many different forms. Be open, acknowledging, and grateful.
5. As ideas come, pay attention to how they "feel."
6. Once an idea creates a strong emotion (either excitement or fear), commit to taking action on it as soon as possible.
7. Follow the energy of the project. If "all systems are go," keep moving forward. If huge resistance is encountered, let it go. Have patience for gestation. Be on the lookout for a new way through.
8. Know that personal issues and beliefs may get in the way. Clear them up. If there is something that you truly want, but it is not being manifested in your life, it is only because you are blocking it. Look at why you might be afraid to have what you say you want. What might you lose by having it? You always have what you want in your life, so something internally has to change to let in your new desire.
9. As personal issues are cleared out of the way, the next nudge towards the dream appears. Keep moving forward.
10. Keep dreaming. Keep having a fascinating experience of life.

Creation Process

Your Past Experiences
Create
Your Memories and Imprints on the Mind
Which Create
Your Beliefs
Which Create
Your Daily Thoughts
Which Create
Your Feelings and Energetic Vibration
That Create
Your Choices
And Create
Your Actions
And Create
Your Results
That Create
Your Past Experiences

Master Mind Group

1. **I SURRENDER**

   I admit that, apart from a Higher Power, I do not have the power to solve my problems, to improve my life. I need help.

2. **I BELIEVE**

   I come to believe that only in my oneness with a Higher Power, or "Master Mind," can I truly change my life.

3. **I AM READY TO BE CHANGED**

   I realize that erroneous, self-defeating thinking is the cause of my problems, unhappiness, fears, and failures. I am ready to have my beliefs and attitudes changed so my life can be transformed.

4. **I DECIDE TO BE CHANGED**

   I make a decision to surrender my will and my life to a Higher Power. I ask to be changed at depth

5. **I FORGIVE**

   I forgive myself for all my mistakes and shortcomings. I also forgive all other people who appear to have harmed me.

6. **I ASK**

   I make known my specific requests, asking my partners' support in knowing that a Higher Being is fulfilling my needs. (Partners may respond with affirmation such as: "I know that you have been heard and you will experience your demonstration.")

7. **I GIVE THANKS**

I give thanks that a Higher Power is responding to my needs and I feel the joy of my requests being fulfilled right now.

8. **I DEDICATE MY LIFE**

I now have a covenant in which it is agreed that a Higher Power is supplying me with an abundance of all things necessary to live a successful and happy life. I dedicate myself to be of maximum service to a Higher Power and to those around me, to live in a manner that sets the highest example for others to follow, and to remain responsive to the Universe's guidance.

I go forth with a spirit of enthusiasm, excitement, and expectancy. I am at peace.

Be Your Own Cheerleader

Are you a reward in yourself—not just for what you do, but also for who you are? While we often crave acknowledgement and love from others, it is what we tell ourselves that creates our truth. I have found that even a few kind and supportive words, said to myself, are a real reward. Becoming my own cheerleader has opened the door for others to champion me as well. Remember that the way in which others treat us is a reflection of the way we treat ourselves.

Stand in front of a mirror. Look into your own eyes. Tell yourself what you appreciate about yourself—out loud. Take your time. Let each self appreciation sink in. At a minimum, share four or five things that you appreciate about yourself. End with telling yourself "I love you." It is a lovely way to start or finish your day. Start seeing the effects reflected back to you in your life.

Also pay attention to the things that you say to and about yourself throughout the day. Are you increasing or lowering your vibration? What about treating yourself to little gifts?

If you only reward yourself for doing well, you are building a foundation for "conditional love." This is where we only give love and acknowledgement for achieving and doing. It creates a do-do-doer. Perhaps you know of a few workaholics. Perhaps you are one. Conditional love creates the belief that you are only worthy of love if you are achieving. That continues into the belief that "if I fail or rest, I am no longer loveable." Give yourself love and rewards for who you are! Give to yourself each and every day!

Forgive and Let Go

Here is a visualization exercise for forgiveness and letting go. Find a quiet space where you will not be disturbed. Close your eyes. Relax and breathe deeply for a minimum of ten breaths before beginning the visualization. Relax some more. Gentle, instrumental music in the background may help you relax. If you record the meditation in your own voice it will deepen your experience. Go slowly and let yourself get truly involved with each scene.

Imagine the person you believe has harmed you standing in front of you. See a black line that connects you to that person. In your mind's eye, have a conversation with them. Ask them how they felt about the situation. Ask them how it affected their lives. Ask them how they are today and if it still affects them. Tell them how it hurt you. Tell them how it affected your life and how it continues to affect you today. Tell them any ways you have secretly been punishing them. Tell them what you wished had happened. Tell them what you have learned. Offer your forgiveness. Tell them that you both have to move past this in your lives. Tell them what you need to move on. See them giving it to you. Tell them that you are sorry for punishing them for so long with your anger. Cut the black line that keeps you attached. Offer your forgiveness. Imagine the two of you sharing a hug or handshake. Then say goodbye and truly wish them well.

Now, imagine yourself locked in a cage, locked in irons. See how helpless you look, how much pain you are in. Now, with the kindness and heart of an angel, see the person you are now going over to that cage, opening the door, and unlocking the chains. Show compassion. Speak loving words to your tortured self. Forgive yourself for holding on to so much anger and for any revenge you may have taken. You have punished yourself enough. Let yourself out of jail and allow your poor battered soul to be bathed in white light. Bring that vision into your heart. When you can feel tenderness, you have done the exercise.

You may want to repeat this exercise whenever you notice that you are feeling angry about something. You will feel freer and lighter when it is done. You will be free to move on in your life.

Giving And Receiving Meditation

Here is a meditation that I use to increase my ability to receive. When I am open to receive what is true for others to give, I magically have fewer needs and wants. I feel more fulfilled. As I receive, I naturally have more to truly give. As I truly give, I open to receive even more. Even though meditation is an inner journey, I absolutely guarantee that you will start to see similar results in your outer world.

Go to a quiet place where you will not be interrupted. Play soft instrumental music if that helps you relax. Close your eyes. Relax. Take a minimum of ten long, deep breaths. Relax even more with every exhalation. Imagine a white line of energy coming through the top of your head, joining you with Heaven. Imagine another white line of energy flowing up through your feet, anchoring you to the Earth. See both energy strands filling you with love and peace. You are receiving from Heaven and from Earth and you are filled.

See your heart opening and the white energy flowing out into the world. One at a time, let the people of your life appear in your mind's eye. Look deep into their eyes and send your white light from your heart to theirs. This white light is your wish to send them love. You may wish to send them other blessings as well. Please feel free to do so. Then see that they are also sending you their white blessing of love. Be open to intuit if they are also sending you other blessings. Thank them and allow the next person to appear.

See your mother, your father, each of your siblings, your partner, your children, your friends, and anyone else who appears in your mind's eye. (I often work with many of my clients when doing this exercise.) When you feel complete with this portion, allow yourself to see them all as a group. See your white energy of love surrounding them and protecting them. Now, feel them sending you their white energy of love to surround and protect you.

As you go through the day, you can do a short form of this visualization. With practice, you will be able to be connected to Heaven in a heartbeat. Just open your heart, send the white line of energy, and share a blessing with someone. It will come back to you in ways you could never have imagined. You can also use this meditation to open your heart and receive whatever dream or goal you desire.

Integration Process for Dilemmas and Conflicts (Finding Energetic Balance)

This is a great exercise to use when working with dilemmas and conflicting beliefs, with others or within yourself. I find it very helpful to prepare for any communication that might create resolution. Close your eyes. Take ten slow, deep breaths. Imagine that you are connected to the Universe with a band of white light. Now imagine that you are also connected to the Earth energetically. Imagine and feel the energy coming up through your legs, filling your body, arms, and head. Then "see" the energy leaving through the top of your head. Now reverse that and see the Universal energy come into the top of your head, travel through and fill your body, and exit out the bottom of your feet. Think about the situation that is concerning you. Ask to be brought to your centre and feel balanced. Move your hands approximately three feet apart. Turn your palms up. Imagine one side of the dilemma or conflict as a ball (of energy) in your left hand. What colour is it? Feel the weight of it. Now imagine putting the other side of the dilemma or conflict in your right hand. Again, imagine it as a ball. What colour is this ball? Feel the weight of it. Compare its weight to the other ball in your left hand. With a ball still attached to each hand, turn your palms so that they face each other. Slowly begin to move your hands together. Think of the question you are looking to answer. Be open to hear any internal messages as you do this. Keep in touch with the feeling of energy in each palm. Do you feel any resistance between the two hands as you slowly bring them together? Gently integrate the energy of both sides as you clasp your hands together. Now that the energies have been brought together, bring your hands to your heart chakra . Relax and breathe. Be willing to find the true answers that will bring you balance. If you have not received a better resolution during this process, watch for it in your thoughts over the next few days. It will come.

Grounding Exercise

All that you need to do to ground your energy is to imagine (as you work with this more, you will eventually be able to feel) the energy coming from the Earth and entering your body from the middle of your feet. Imagine and feel that energy coming up through your legs, filling your body, arms, and head. Then visualize the energy leaving through the top of your head. Now reverse that, see Universal energy coming into the top of your head, travelling through and filling your body, and exiting out the bottom of your feet. There are many different techniques for grounding, but this is a quick one that works for me. Grounding helps stop the thoughts that take your attention from what is happening in the present moment. Grounding clears your mind of clutter. When you are fully grounded and present, you will be much more conscious of things in your surroundings, and your intuition will be enhanced. This way you are more capable of dealing with any potholes on your journey. When you can see what is coming, you are less likely to be side swiped or have an accident.

100 Yearly Goals—Using the Law of Attraction

Each New Year's Day, I start my annual list of 100 things I want. These are huge, grandiose goals. I do not have the faintest idea of how I can achieve them. I give them over to the Universe to create. It is an exercise to expand both my ability to see greater possibilities (stretch my limited thinking) and increase my ability to receive. These are goals that I declare I am open to achieving. In truth, what I am doing is expanding my energy field—my magnetism. These are goals that I want to attract without putting in any conscious effort.

I write them out as affirmations. I write them out as positive, elaborate statements phrased in current time. For example: when I wanted to earn $100,000 per year, I wrote, "I now earn far in excess of $100,000 per year, with ease and grace." When I wanted to be a more loving person, I wrote: "I have an open heart that allows me to bless myself and every person with gifts of love." Who do you want to be? What do you want to have? What do you want to do? Take your thoughts of being, doing, and having and turn them into grandiose, positive statements phrased as though you have already achieved them. The more emotion in these statements, the better. Emotion is the energy of attraction, so really feel it.

Write out 100 of these statements and put them away. I look at my list only about three times a year, and only for the purpose of checking off the goals that I know have arrived in my life. Without any conscious effort on my part, I average between a 60-80% rate of achievement each year.